Wag Wars

THE GLAMOUR STORY OF FOOTBALLERS' WIVES

Sam Kimberley

GIBSON SQUARE

First published in the UK by Gibson Square in 2021

UK Tel: +44 (0)20 7096 1100
US Tel: +1 646 216 9813

rights@gibsonsquare.com
www.gibsonsquare.com

ISBN 9781783342150

*Papers used by Gibson Square are natural, recyclable products made from wood grown
in sustainable forests; inks used are vegetable based. Manufacturing conforms to ISO
14001, and is accredited to FSC and PEFC chain of custody schemes. Colour-printing
is through a certified CarbonNeutral® company that offsets its CO2 emissions.*

Printed by CPI.

Contents

Wags of Yore

Footballers have always had wives and girlfriends. But back in the days of leather balls and Dubbined boots, they stayed at home, making tea and washing his muddy kit. Tom Finney, a veteran of that era, is still reputed to be one of football's greatest players, scoring 187 goals during his fourteen-year stint with Preston North End, along with thirty for England. When he married Elsie Noblett in 1945, there were no paparazzi outside the church and nor were there magazines like *OK!* or *Hello!* to snap up the rights.

'Elsie and I got married in the local church and had our reception at St Jude's Hall in Preston, the place we'd met at a Saturday night dance a few years before,' he recalled. 'There was nothing in the papers… Elsie worked at a Preston steam laundry. I think we went to Blackpool for our honeymoon.'

They were married for fifty-nine years until her death in November 2004 and had two children.

'I only earned 12s/10d a week as a footballer back then and I don't remember how much our wedding cost,' he said. 'It was definitely peanuts. But the most important thing was for Elsie and I to be married, and I miss her terribly.'

His weekly wage of 12 shilling and ten old pence—that's 64p—is worth £28 now, so there was little for Elsie to splash out on Gucci and Versace.

Before becoming one of Manchester United most famous managers, Tommy Docherty also played for Preston North End and Scotland. He married his first wife Agnes in a low-key ceremony at the Sacred Heart Church in Girvan, South Ayrshire, on 27 December 1949. The day after the wedding, the newlyweds caught the train to Preston—Tommy had transferred there from Celtic for £2,000 and a weekly wage of £8.

He concentrated on his footballing career while she stayed at home to look after their four children. But in 1977, after twenty-seven years of marriage, Tommy announced in a tabloid that he was having an affair with Mary Brown, the wife of Man U's physio. At matches the crowd then sung a spiced-up version of 'Knees Up Mother Brown'.

He and Agnes divorced and he married Mary, having two more children with her. A private person, Agnes did not go blabbing to the press. She was adamant that her story should not be told until after her death. She died of a heart attack in 2002 and in 2008 her son Thomas Junior published *Married to a Man of Two Halves* in 2008. This was based on memoirs and newspaper cuttings which he had discovered when clearing out his mother's house.

'My mum died with a broken heart,' he explained. 'She never got over Dad, he was the love of her life. He married the woman he had an affair with and I believe they have just celebrated their twenty-fifth wedding anniversary. I haven't spoken to him since he left Mum, but how many people can claim two silver weddings in their lifetime?'

Then playing for Chelsea, Jimmy Greaves was already on his way to become the First Division's top scorer when he married Irene Barden at Romford registry office in Essex in 1958. They were both eighteen. He was earning £8 a week during the season and £7 a week in summer. Their first home was a flat in the clubhouse inside Wimbledon's old Plough Lane football ground. Despite being Chelsea's star player and signing for England in 1959, money was still tight and the pair supplemented their income by weeding Wimbledon's terraces for £8 a week, taking the Greaves' summer wage to £15 a week.

They had four children. Like several contemporary football players, he succumbed to alcoholism and they separated for three months in 1977. He then gave up the booze and renewed their vows forty years later in 2017. After retiring from the game, he ran a packaging company and became a TV football pundit.

A forerunner of David and Victoria Beckham, and Ashley and Cheryl Cole, legendary England captain

Billy Wright married pop star Joy Beverley, a singer with the girl group the Beverley Sisters, at Poole register office on 27 July 1958, in what was dubbed the first celebrity footballer wedding. Although they had decided to marry in the quiet Dorset town of Poole in an attempt to give the press the slip, the fans turned out in their thousands.

'When we arrived at the register office, there were six or seven thousand people outside,' Billy said in his autobiography. 'We lost the aerial of our car and on the way through the crowds one of the bridesmaids lost her shoe! We attended a small luncheon afterwards before driving to Stratford-on-Avon for the shortest honeymoon ever. Twenty four-hours later, Joy was working in Bournemouth and I resumed training with Wolves!'

Joy's sister Teddie recalled: 'It was a very informal affair. Billy came on his own on the train to Bournemouth and walked to our house from the station. We drove to the register office from there. It was a very quiet affair, but very happy.... There were no gifts, no fuss at all, it was just love from beginning to end. The important thing is that the love lasts, not the dress.'

The couple were married for thirty-six years until Billy's death from stomach cancer in 1994, aged seventy. By then, the age of innocence was over. In 1960, the maximum wage for professional footballers was set by the Football League at £20 a week, worth £450 a week now, just fifty per cent more than the average working man. The following year, in the face of a threatened strike by the players, the Football League abolished the maximum wage.

Since then, TV money has poured into football. Transfer fees are in eight figures and players earn hundreds of thousands of pounds a week. Top WAGs—wives and girlfriends—can expect to live in a £1-million mansion, be swathed in designer labels and travel in stretch limos and private jets.

Has it made them happier? You'll find out below. But WAGs now have their own 'premier league' and draw about as much media attention as the beautiful game. Every year the media draw up rankings of the most beautiful WAGs, or the richest, or the hottest, or best-dressed, or with the biggest house. The press tracks carefully who wins battles on the beach with the skimpiest bikinis and the best tans all year round.

And now there is money to be made by running to the tabloids every time something goes wrong in their relationship or with other WAGs. When things do go wrong, the media is there to record the most explosive feuds, declaring winners and losers. Girls Aloud singer Cheryl Tweedy had a much-publicised split up with ex-husband Ashley Cole. Graeme Souness' first and second wives faced each other down in a vicious court battle. Even Posh and Becks—David and Victoria

Beckham —have had their troubles. But Paul Gascoigne—Gazza—and his wife Sheryl's endless on-again off-again relationship takes the biscuit. His fall from soccer superstar into shambling alcoholism while her ascent to media stardom, after surviving domestic violence at his hands, was played out, blow by blow, in the press. WAGs are no longer forgotten in the shadows but are public figures in their own right.

1
In the Wag-ground

Following Tottenham Hotspurs' double, winning both the League and the FA Cup in 1961, a book called *The Double: The Inside Story of Spurs' Triumphant 1960-61 Season* was published which, in passing, mentioned the doings of the players' wives. There were really only Ws and not yet WAGs, as the girlfriends stayed well in the background. Eight of the first team were married. On a Saturday night, they would get together with their husbands and invited guests in Tottenham's Buttery Bar.

On match days the women would meet in the ladies' room in the club, where they would chat over tea and sandwiches before moving to the stands to watch their husband's play. There was a bar, but their intake of alcohol was strictly limited. This was left to the men who would be drinking whisky and smoking cigars in the boardroom. This was out-of-bounds for women until 1959 when pneumatic Hollywood movie star Jayne Mansfield visited White Hart Lane. The players were invited to have a drink with her while the wives were kept at arms' length. There was even some flirtation. Mansfield told centre-forward Bobby Smith: 'You've got lovely legs.' Smith replied: 'And you've got a lovely bust.'

Some of the wives did not join in the inner circle. Captain Danny Blanchflower's wife Betty did not go to the matches, especially on Saturdays, staying home with the kids as a housewife. Occasionally though, she took potluck with babysitters. She said she got on quite well with the other wives and girlfriends. However, she said: 'There was always a bit of jealousy because Danny was a transferred player and got a better house.'

He had been transferred from Aston Villa to Spurs for £30,000 in 1954 and was voted Footballer of the Year in 1958 and 1961.

Manager Bill Nicholson's wife Darkie stayed at home looking after their two little girls and cooking an after-match dinner.

Full back Ray Evans' future wife Sandra didn't mix with the other women either. She felt that there was some resentment towards her because her dad was assistant manager.

'A lot of them were married with kids and I had only just left school,' she said.

She got on better with the players, meeting bachelors Peter Baker, John White and Terry Dyson at a dance hall called the Tottenham Royal. Some of the married players also went there.

'A crowd of them used to go,' she said. 'The married ones didn't bring their wives, but it was harmless fun. We'd dance the twist and rock 'n' roll. A Spurs fan called Dave Greenaway, a sort of male groupie about my dad's age, used to come and pick up myself, Lynn, who became Peter Baker's wife, and a few others. He'd take us to the Royal and bring us home afterwards. The supporters do a lot when they like a team.'

Tottenham's 1960's WAGs were demure, but things were about to change. In 1961 Johnny Haynes, captain of Fulham and England, became the first £100-a-week player—now worth £2,250 a week. He also had a lucrative side-line as a 'Brylcreem boy', advertising the hair grooming product as players do now.

Since then the money has skyrocketed. In 1979 Nottingham Forest became the first club to buy a player for £1 million, signing Trevor Francis. They also paid Peter Shilton £1,200 a week, making him the best paid player in the country.

By 1994, Chris Sutton was being paid £10,000 a week by Blackburn. Sol Campbell demanded £100,000 a week to play for Arsenal. In 2010 Carlos Tevez became the first player to earn £1 million per month, or £286,000 a week, when he signed for Manchester City. Five years later Cristiano Ronaldo was being paid £15 million a year, after tax, by Real Madrid. In 2020, he was being paid £53 million by Juventus, plus £35 million in endorsements. But he had been overtaken by Lionel Messi who earned £95 million.

That is not to say that the WAGs were after money. Some, such as Victoria Beckham and Cheryl Tweedy, have lucrative careers of their own. They followed in the footsteps of Joy Beverley who earned considerably more than her husband, Wolverhampton and England captain Billy Wright, while the League's wage cap was still in place. But these days a little extra cash, especially when counted in the millions, couldn't harm. Besides, players these days are better groomed and a lot fitter. According to a poll conducted a few years ago by *More* magazine, now every six in ten women dreams of being a WAG.

2
The Best Wag

In the 1960s many of the players still smoked. The older ones had seen service during World War II. But that generation were bowing out and the young were taking over. Emblematic of this was George Best who, in 1963, made his debut in a Man-U shirt. With his good looks and lavish lifestyle, he quickly became a celebrity, known as '*El Quinto Beatle*'—'The Fifth Beatle'—after scoring two early goals in an historic victory against Portugal's Benfica at their Stadium of Light in 1966. And there were girlfriends—lots of them.

'I spent a lot of money on booze, birds and fast cars. The rest I just squandered,' he said famously. He did try to reign it in though.

'In 1969 I gave up women and alcohol,' he said. 'It was the worst twenty minutes of my life.'

In a more reflective mood, Best said: 'I had a tremendous amount of relationships because I suppose I was in a position to. I had plenty of money and I went to the sort of functions where there were always plenty of beautiful women around.'

A former agent recalled: 'Women just flocked on him like bees on honey.'

Some of them were very high-profile. They included *Carry On* star Barbara Windsor, Miss Great Britain Carolyn Moore and two Miss Worlds—Marjorie Wallace and Mary Stavin. When he was found in a hotel suite with a naked beauty queen and £15,000 in cash strewn across his bed, by a porter, the man asked: 'Where did it all go wrong, George?'

Best was unapologetic.

'I used to go missing a lot... Miss Canada, Miss United Kingdom, Miss World,' he said.

But he insisted his reputation was over-rated.

'They say I slept with seven Miss Worlds,' he said. 'I didn't. It was only four. I didn't turn up for the other three.'

By way of an explanation, in a drunken chat show appearance in 1990, he told Terry Wogan: 'I like screwing.'

It was definitely preferable to playing football.

'If you'd given me the choice of going out and beating four men and smashing a goal in from thirty yards against Liverpool or going to bed with Miss World, it would have been a difficult choice,' he said. 'Luckily, I had both.'

However, on a particular occasion when he missed

a match to spend time with an actress. The fans were not pleased.

Asked how close to kick-off he'd ever had sex, he replied: 'Er… I think it was half-time.'

As well as being rich, fit and good-looking, he was also attentive. One old girlfriend said: 'Whenever George looked at you, you felt you were the only woman in the world.'

In 1978, he married model and former *Playboy* Bunny Angie MacDonald-Janes at the Candlelight Wedding Chapel in Las Vegas. The priest officiating wore a lime-green suit. According to Angie, George's manager Ken Adams had sold the story and picture rights to a tabloid newspaper, so on the flight from Los Angeles they could not even sit next together in case other papers were alerted.

In the chapel, George found he'd forgotten or lost the wedding ring and had to borrow one from his best man, Bobby McAlinden, a teammate at the Los Angeles Aztecs. At their reception, a waitress split Coke down Angie's white jacket.

After the couple flew back to Los Angeles, Angie recalled: 'I thought some romance could be salvaged when I saw George disappearing into the bedroom and getting undressed.'

However, her expectations were dashed when he announced he was changing to go out drinking with his mates. His last words to his crestfallen bride on her wedding night were: 'Don't wait up.'

Then there was the pressure from the media to deal with. Asif Kapadia, a British filmmaker who has made the Grammy and Oscar winning documentary 'Amy', about Amy Winehouse, said: 'If you look at all the headlines George Best generated, he was used and abused, belittled... When I saw Amy and I saw the paparazzi camped outside [her home], all those scenes, the wide shots of the press, you hounding her, it was probably fifty times worse than what George Best faced, but George Best was the first one to have faced that.'

Indeed, by the 80s, Best he was in the grip of raging alcoholism.

Angie, who opened a bar called Bestie's with George, recalled: 'If 70,000 men wanted to have one drink with George, they had one drink. George had 70,000.'

She thought she could keep on the straight and narrow by giving him a settled home life.

'You keep thinking that you can fix it and that all he needs is a nice home-cooked meal and nice house and to settle down but it never quite works like that when there's alcohol involved,' she said.

They struggled on for eight years. One night she was driving home from a doctor's appointment with their son Calum when she saw what she took to be a down-and-out stumbling down the middle of the road.

'This poor man is all hunched over, soaking wet and I think oh my God, that poor homeless tramp and then I realise... it is my husband, drunk as a skunk, walking down the road, soaking wet,' she said.

It was George staggering home from another bender. She did not stop to pick him up.

'I realised it was over. I always wanted to look after him but enough is enough, I can't look after both babies, the big one's got to go,' she said. 'After that, George drank every single day for thirty years.'

And when, in 2000, Patsy Kensit played her in the biopic *Best*, Angie was incensed.

'I haven't been consulted at all, even though it shows my life,' she said.

Striking back, she wrote *George and Me: My Autobiography*. Its hook line was: 'I didn't realise that six years of marriage would last a lifetime.' After they split she said that she continued to try offering support and advice to help him conquer his alcoholism. Despite everything George had put her through with his drunken antics, she claimed in the book: 'I remain good friends with George. He is the only man I ever loved.'

Returning to Los Angeles, Angie built a career as a fitness trainer, producing and starring in her own workout videos, and starring on television in shows and series for Sky TV. She coached celebrity clients, including Cher, Sharon Stone and Daryl Hannah and she wrote a series of books for women over forty, including one about the menopause called *A Change for the Best.*

In 2017, Angie joined her son Calum Best on the nineteenth series of *Celebrity Big Brother,* which she entered as a new contestant. She was first to be evicted on day eleven after receiving nominations from singer and TV presenter Coleen Nolan and glamour model Nicola McLean, star of Channel Five's *Generation Sex* and *WAGS' World... with Nicola McLean* on Wedding TV, after she married footballer Tom Williams in 2009. Calum Best has become somewhat of a reality star in his own right, winning the 2nd season of *Celebrity Love Island* on ITV in 2006, looking for love on *E4's Celebs Go Dating* and feuding with exes on MTV's *Ex on the Beach* in 2020. Calum has also struggled with drinking and drugs.

But George, despite previous efforts to stop, did not give up drinking—or glamorous women. In 1995, he married ex-air hostess Alex Pursey in a ceremony in the Royal Borough of Kensington and Chelsea. She was twenty-seven years his junior and they met in a night club when she was twenty-one years old. They were together for twelve years.

'I'm not even a football person—I'm more into rugby—but watching George play was like watching magic,' she said. 'And, of course, he did have a colourful life off the pitch; he was a good-looking guy... the first world superstar of his type. You can see why people are still interested. It's a good—if cautionary—story.'

The affair did not start out well. Calum claimed that George attacked him when he was just fourteen after accusing him of having an affair with Alex. He had returned home to his London flat to find his son playing cards with his fiancée.

'You're not my f****** son,' George had roared.

Recalling how his dad accused him of 'getting together' with Alex, Calum said: 'Dad is in a bad state. He has messy, shaggy hair, his face is swollen and the skin on his hands and cheeks and forehead is red and peeling. Jesus, Dad, I think, you don't look so well.

'There's a pause as he looks around. I see his eyes and they're blazing. 'What the f*** is going on here?' he snaps. He's not just angry, he's raging. I look at Alex and she's terrified.'

In his autobiography *Second Best: My Dad and Me*, Callum wrote: 'I realise what he must be thinking. My drunk, old, alcohol-poisoned dad is convinced his four-teen-year-old son and his beautiful young fiancée are getting it on behind his back.

'I try to take control of the situation. 'Dad,' I speak calmly, 'Chill out. This really is not what you think.'

"F*** off, you piece of s***,' he shouts. 'F*** off. You're not my f***ing son.'

'Dad is staring at me with hatred in his eyes. 'Don't you lie to me,' he snarls, stepping closer. 'You're not my son, you f***ing piece of s**t.'

'And boom! — his right hand whips up to my throat. The back of my head hits the wall, his hand tightens around my neck and my feet lift up off the ground.

'And then he lets me go. I'm rasping, coughing, trying to get air down my neck. I see his hand drop down to his side and then whack, up it comes and he backhands me across the right side of my head, knocking me over.

'"You're not my son," he shouts again. "You're not even meant to be. I hate you."'

Calum also recalled his father leaving him alone in a Manchester hotel room aged eleven while he went to see a hooker. On another occasion he recalled how his father had kissed him.

'I am about to start trying to go back to sleep when Dad rolls over, puts his face in front of mine and kisses me: as in, he puts his tongue in my mouth. That kind of kiss,' he said. 'I freeze. What's going on? I'm old enough to know what a French kiss is. But why is Dad doing it to me?

'Years later, when I start drinking heavily myself, I work out what happened. He got home so out of his head that when he saw my long, blond hair in his bed he assumed it was a girl and did the obvious thing of kissing her, because he thought that's what she was there for.'

Then there was the rare occasion when father and son played football, only for Calum to discover that this display of paternal affection was a publicity stunt.

'At the end of the session the photographer gives Dad a brown paper bag full of what looks like thousands of pounds,' Calum said. 'We go to the pub and he gives me some to spend, probably because he feels guilty about using me like that.'

But Alex was not to be discouraged.

'He was down to earth, he was cheeky, he was lovely,' she said. He had a heart of gold. 'He was funny, generous—he was just a perfect husband, apart from the alcohol.'

Alex became a successful model, named female Rear of the Year in 2004. That year, she took part in series three of *I'm a Celebrity… Get Me Out of Here!* and was fourth to be voted out. That same year, she and George split. Neither appeared at the hearing and the divorce went through in two minutes twenty seconds. Months later he died when the immuno-suppressive drugs he took after a liver transplant led to him having a kidney transplant. Alex visited him on his death bed.

'I went to see him just before he died, and he was unconscious,' she recalled. 'I just said, 'I love you and always will, and I'm sorry for what's happened."

Best had achieved the sort of fame no footballer had before him. He appeared in TV ads and played himself in a cameo role in the 1971 British comedy film

Percy. Irish actor and novelist John Lynch played him in the movie *Best* and money poured in.

Indie rock band, *The Wedding Present*, called their first album *George Best*. It featured him on the cover wearing his red Man-U kit. After his death, Brian Kennedy and Peter Corry released a single called 'George Best—A Tribute'. George featured in EA Sports' FIFA video game series; he was included as an icon in the FIFA 19 Ultimate Team Legends. His overall rating stood at 93, behind Maradona at 95 and Pele at 97.

Two years after he died, the magazine *GQ* named him as one of The Fifty Most Stylish Men of the Last Fifty years. They wrote: 'Before Becks there was Best. The dark-haired boy wonder from Belfast hijacked English football when he debuted for Manchester United in 1963, becoming a soccer sensation, celebrity, and sex symbol in short order. Whether it was his Beatles-inspired haircut, slim suits, or Chelsea boots, his style reflected and defined the times. He always kept current, from the crisp lines of mod to the rococo collars and peak lapels of '70s London. Bestie inspired the 1966 Kinks classic 'Dedicated Follower of Fashion,' and as his legend grew, his life came to revolve less around the pitch than discotheques and parties....'

In 2012, he posthumously appeared in the list of The New Elizabethans to mark the diamond Jubilee of Queen Elizabeth II. He was described by the selection panel as a person 'whose actions during the reign of Elizabeth II have had a significant impact on lives in these islands and given the age its character'.

However, there was a dark side to being one of George Best's wives. In their divorce in 1986, Angie cited domestic violence. Alex also claimed that he had hit her in the face on more than one occasion in his authorised biography *Bestie*. The book went on to reveal that that he had struck another of his girlfriends at least once and had been arrested and charged with assault on a waitress, Stevie Sloniecka, in November 1972, fracturing her nose in Reuben's nightclub in Manchester. He was successfully defended when the case reached court in January 1973 by his drinking buddy George Carman QC.

A post-mortem catfight broke out when Alex claimed that their former house in Kingswood, Surrey, was haunted on *This Morning*. Cynics suggested that the remarks were the upshot of 'the other ex-Mrs Best'—Angie—hogging the limelight following her stint, with son Calum, on *Celebrity Big Brother*. Alex was doing a pilot for a TV show called *Unbelievable* where it was concluded that the ghost was not George's but that of a former resident named Tom.

Meanwhile she became ambassador for LA Skincare.

'I'm opening beauticians and promoting their products, which is very nice. You get lots of nice creams and things, which is lovely,' she said. At the age of forty-five, she also admitted using Botox.

'I've been having Botox since I was about twenty-eight,' she said. 'I only do it once every year—and sometimes I've gone for maybe three years at a time without it.

'I started doing it very, very young because I didn't want to get lines from smiling, so it was preventative. That's the only thing I've ever had done—apart from my boobs.'

Alex was not upset by the mention she got in Calum's autobiography.

'Calum has every right to say what he wants about his father,' she said. 'I've written an autobiography so I'm not going to throw stones at glass houses. If you are doing an autobiography you've got to be brutally honest, otherwise there's no point in writing one.'

She also admitted bumping into Calum from time to time. Her new footballing favourite was Cristiano Ronaldo, but she worried about the new generation of young, gifted players who often get too much, too soon.

'When they're kids and get all that adulation, which is what happened with George, I don't think they know what to do next because football's such a major part of their lives,' she said.

In her autobiography *Always Alex*, she claimed she was no gold-digger. When they wed George he was pretty well broke, selling off the medals he'd won, and their first married residence was his dive of a flat in Chelsea, where she had to wash her knickers by hand in the sink. She also said the tabloid's criticised her for encouraging his alcoholism, simply for being photographed holding a glass of wine when he was trying to quit the drink, while journalists took him out and got him drunk for days on end.

She also confessed another on-off relationship with footballer John Scales.

'His team-mates started to call him 'Gigolo'— unfortunately, it took me a while to cotton on to the full significance of that nickname,' she said.

In her book, she also addressed the question of domestic violence, saying that once Best had broken her arm in a brawl—though she had gone back to him afterwards.

'The only good thing to come out of it was that I had the excuse to have my hair washed and blow-dried at the hairdressers twice a week, a real indulgence. Well, I told myself, I think I deserve a little treat!' she said.

On other occasions, he beat her and cut off much of her hair while drunk, but still she stuck by him. Towards the end, after she had nursed him through and past his liver transplant, draining the bile from his tube with plastic gloves and a measuring jug, and tried to sort out his shambolic finances, he went on a few benders and disappeared off with other women and ended up in the papers again.

'I couldn't quite believe the things I'd put up with,' she said. 'The way they came round time and again, and I'd do the same. You're always hoping. Always. Until one day, if you're lucky, you manage to stop.'

She tried to get him into therapy.

'George wouldn't hear of it. He's actually an extremely shy man, and never wanted to deal with it in that kind of confrontational way, and that's why it was never dealt with; it just seemed to go away some times, possibly because those times he was almost dead.'

Then, when she thought he had stopped, she would find a tell-tale bottle—once hidden in a pile of chopped wood—knowing it would be a matter of hours before she'd find him surrounded by empties, in his bed or in a park or in a ditch. Or she'd have to go traipsing round Chelsea pubs, begging people to stop killing him. People would buy him a drink, just so they could say 'I bought George Best a drink.' And he'd never refuse.

'One thing I realised is that the more I tried to stop him, to tell him to stop, the more he would resent me, and seek an excuse to start a row to get away. It's a grim situation: the more that you, one person who truly loves and wants to help, try to love him and help an alcoholic, the less they want to be with you,' she told Euan Ferguson of the *Guardian*.

Alex did not follow his passion.

'I remember him telling me about the football. I've

never really got or understood football, and didn't fall for George because he was an idol or anything; I fell for him because he was charming George. But he would tell me how he'd practise with both feet, anywhere, at any time, determined to be the best not on one foot but on both feet. There was no option in his mind but to be stubborn, to be the best. And once that passed, I've thought: he had to be the best at drinking instead. Had to be the best at keeping bars open. Preferably the dirtiest bars: if you had a line of pubs, wine bars, gastropubs in any street, you knew you'd find George in the filthiest old man's pub at the end, with the sticky carpet.'

There was nothing glamorous about things. He suffered from swollen feet that left him hobbling, unable to walk up hills on holiday. His swollen testicles led to the lack of any sex life. And the shakes, only occasionally 'because most of the time he never got a hangover; he simply topped up'.

Throughout her twenties she would often cry herself to sleep. However, she forgave him.

'I don't really resent it, resent George, at all, because we also had a great time together,' she said. 'He gave me a good life, too, often a really good life. The good times.'

3
Wag to Riches

Tina Moore (neé Dean) is said to be the first true WAG. She was the wife of Bobby Moore, the only England captain to raise the Jules Trophy when England won the FIFA World Cup in 1966. They met in the Palais nightclub in Ilford in 1957. She was fifteen; he was seventeen and a trainee at West Ham earning £8 a week. They danced to 'Blue Moon'.

'I was not overly impressed at first,' she said. 'He wasn't quite handsome, but he was good-looking, and charm personified.'

She stood him up on their first date, but he was besotted and pursued her relentlessly. She relented after seeing him walking down the street and was encouraged by her mother to invite him round for tea.

At West Ham Moore was the rising star, donning the number six shirt in 1958. No hard-tackling defender, Moore was a world-class reader of the game, anticipating the opponent's moves. He was also a romantic, leaving love letters under Tina's pillow. They married on

30 June 1960. She wore a long white dress topped with sheer lace and her bouquet and floral arrangement centred around orange roses. That year, he was called up for the England Under-23 squad.

The newly-weds moved into a three-bedroom terrace house in Gants Hill, Essex, costing £3,850. In 1961, he was named West Ham Player of the Year. The following year he became captain and made his debut for England's first team in the World Cup in Chile. England was knocked out in the quarter finals by Brazil, but Pelé said Moore was the greatest defender he had ever played against.

Moore was just twenty-three and Tina was expecting their first child, Roberta, when he was diagnosed with testicular cancer.

'It was up to the next of kin to decide whether a patient was told they had cancer. It was a death sentence in those days,' she told the *Sun*. 'I pleaded with the surgeon not to tell him. I was very worried for the baby and for Bobby. I didn't know if he was going to live or die.'

She later told the *Radio Times*: 'The very thought of cancer could affect the healing process. That word was never, ever mentioned between us in all the years we were together.'

However, he had to be told eventually and, fourteen months later, had one of his testicles removed and made a full recovery. They had a son named Dean and

Bobby Moore went on to captain England in the 1966 World Cup, leading the team out for their victory in the finals at Wembley, with Tina cheering him on.

'Bobby had overcome cancer and there he was holding up the cup at the peak of his beauty and his footballing power,' said Tina. 'The whole of England was cheering for him. It was too much to take in. I remember Bobby walking up the steps to receive the trophy wiping his hands. That was typical of him. He wouldn't have wanted to have sullied the Queen's gloves. I was so proud of him. He was my world.'

Tina had her own role to play at the World Cup. She led the England wives on two excursions. One was to the Black and White Minstrel show, the other to the Golders Green shopping centre. Otherwise the players' wives attended the games but were segregated from their men. After the victory they attended a separate dinner. They were re-united after on an excursion to female impersonator Danny La Rue's club, where they were fêted with a rendition of 'When the Saints Come Marching In'.

Afterwards the Moores went on to celebrate at the Playboy club on Park Lane in Mayfair and it wasn't long before the glamorous young couple counted the movie stars and music legends among their closest friends. Sean Connery and his wife were so fond of them they babysat for them while they were in Spain.

Photographs of Tina in an England shirt worn as a

dress in a forest appeared in the pages of newspapers and magazines. Soon designer shops were lending her clothes and taxi drivers would not charge them for rides. But Tina still described herself as 'a Gants Hill housewife' in the press. She and the other footballers' wives were just 'ordinary girls'. Yet she led the 'girls' as they jet-setted to the 1970 Mexico where Bobby was to be briefly held in custody for stealing a bracelet.

Tina Moore (middle) surrounded by the other 'ordinary' girls.

Between them, little had changed. Tina said that outside of the spotlight Bobby was 'very soft and romantic', and he used to leave love notes for her. But when he went out with friends he would turn into 'mischievous, irresponsible Bobby'.

She told the *Radio Times*: 'He never changed—always protective of myself and the children.'

However, Bobby's paycheque doubled and before long they moved into a luxurious Georgian mansion in Chigwell. Tina worked as a model. Like a modern-day WAG she was very fashion conscious and was accused of exploiting her husband's fame, appearing regularly in the press and writing new newspaper columns. She also starred in a TV ad for Bisto.

The couple were so high profile that Tina and their two children were the target of a kidnapping plot in 1970 and there were threats to shoot Bobby during a West Ham game.

In 1973, he moved to Fulham, ending his playing career there in 1977. He then planned to move into management. Elton John had attended the launch of Bobby's autobiography. He was chairman of Watford, then languishing in Division Four and they got together to talk about Bobby taking over as manager.

'They met for lunch and got on well,' said Tina. 'Watford wasn't a big club, but Bobby was intrigued by the challenge and enthused by Elton's ambition to turn it into a major name in football. They discussed terms, shook hands and arranged to meet again to sign a contract. Bobby was buoyant that his career was moving into a fulfilling new phase.'

Meanwhile the Moores set off for a holiday in Majorca and things went 'strangely quiet'. Bobby went out for a run one morning and came back to their hotel with an English newspaper that contained some devastating news. Tina said that her husband 'turned white'.

'I looked at the sports headline. Watford had announced their new manager—Graham Taylor,' Tina said. 'Bobby was lost for words. The breath seemed to have been knocked out of him. At last he said, 'I thought it was a done deal. We shook hands.'

'He'd been looking forward to the job so much. He and Elton John had really clicked.'

While Elton John had been keen to hire Moore, three of Watford's directors expressed concerns that he was not right for the role, having no experience of the Fourth Division. In need of a second opinion, Elton had sought advice from then England manager Don Revie, who recommended future England manager Taylor. Taylor actually turned the approach down at first, but after a personal call from Elton expressing his disappointment, he decided to take up the offer.

Elton had grand ambitions of getting the small club to the top flight and into Europe. When asked by Taylor how much he thought it would cost, Elton replied: 'About a million.' That was good enough for Taylor, who shook hands on a deal with the pop star that would become reality. Under Taylor, Watford made it into the First Division and qualified for the UEFA Cup.

It seems that Bobby never discovered why Elton had changed his mind. It was a significant moment in Moore's life, as his career in football went into a downward spiral from which it would never recover.

'He never found out why he didn't get that job,' said Tina, 'On the face of it he accepted what had happened, but he was terribly hurt and it was a pivotal event in his life. Bobby made it clear to everyone he was looking for work and applied for several managerial vacancies but received knockback after knockback.

'I couldn't understand why he wasn't being given a chance, and nor could he. He was getting by making personal appearances and doing a few football-related jobs, but it was a proper role he wanted. As the months rolled past and nothing came, the newspapers began to ask, "What's wrong with Bobby Moore?"'

Having missed out on the Watford manager's job, he was besieged with money problems, which led to depression. He had spells managing non-league Oxford City, a club in the Danish Third Division and the Eastern AA in Hong Kong. When he returned in 1982, the couple's financial situation had become perilous.

'When he came back from Hong Kong he shook for two days. That's not normal,' Tina said. 'He was crying all the time. He was in a terrible, terrible situation. Looking back, he was obviously deeply depressed. He couldn't get a job. He had no money. It was dreadful for him.'

She said, 'He first changed when the football finished, and he couldn't get a job. It was outrageous how the FA treated him, a scandal. It's all very well that there are statues to him now, but that should have happened during his lifetime. He was very proud, and felt rejected, bewildered.'

The downturn in his career an obstacle that he could not overcome.

'I could see that the man was being torn apart,' she added. 'He was wondering what the hell was going on. Self-doubt started to creep in. Mentally it was a very dreadful thing.'

She believed that the pressure caused Bobby to find solace in the arms of another woman—something Tina was not prepared to put up with.

'He always hated confrontation and would internalise a lot of things. I found to my cost that he would cut off,' she said. 'He could put up a wall and freeze people out. It all contributed to our break-up.'

It was while Bobby was on a visit to Australia that Tina made the fateful phone call that would change both their lives and end their marriage. She called Bobby's hotel room and another woman answered. Tina was devastated.

'He refused to tell me anything about her, but I sensed he was vacillating between the two of us, and I was determined to win him back,' she recalled. 'He, too, was adamant he could work through his problem. But the atmosphere between us grew so icy we could have chilled champagne in it. Eventually he told me he was in love with this other woman. I physically collapsed. I couldn't eat and lost twenty pounds in as many days. I begged, cajoled, lost all my dignity. I reached my lowest point sobbing my story to a stranger on a bus. I thought my world had ended.'

She said Bobby had also been suffering by leading a double life which eventually caught up with him. While insisting that her husband was not a womaniser, she gave him an ultimatum. He left—leaving her heart-broken.

'I was still in love with him,' she said. 'I was devastated. I had been with Bobby for twenty-eight years.'

He took on the job of rebuilding Southend United with some limited success. But his star quality on the pitch didn't translate into the managerial world.

'He existed in a kind of limbo, such a contrast to the golden days of success,' explained Tina. 'What made it really awful was the feeling the football world had cast him into darkness. He became morose, his spirit crushed.'

After some poor business dealings, he joined London radio station Capital Gold as a football commentator. The couple divorced in 1986. Bobby went on to marry Stephanie Parlane, an air hostess nine years his junior, in 1991, just two years before his death from bowel and liver cancer aged just fifty-one.

Three years after their divorce, Tina bumped into Bobby on the London Underground. It would be the last time she would see her ex-husband alive.

'He'd lost his golden glow, still, it was lovely to see him,' she said.

Desperate to escape being seen only as Bobby's first wife, Tina moved to America. Tragically, their son Dean died of natural causes in 2011 aged just forty-three. Tina went on to have a long-term relationship with Irish bar owner Steve Duggan. However, she told the *Daily Telegraph* that she regretted the collapse of her marriage.

'I was flabbergasted. The separation was horrendous. But it was ten years before I stopped being in love with him,' she said.

She wrote her memoir *Bobby Moore: By The Person Who Knew Him Best*. In 2020, this was turned into the three-part TV drama *Tina and Bobby*, starring Michelle Keegan and Lorne MacFadyen, with Tina as script consultant. She also coached Michelle to get her into character, giving her tips and stories from her life.

However, while Tina Moore may have marked the beginning of the WAG phenomenon, others remained outside the limelight. On 23 September 1974, Kevin Keegan married his childhood sweetheart Jean Woodhouse at St Peter's in Chains Roman Catholic Church in his hometown of Doncaster. At twenty-four, he was already a star player for England and Liverpool, who had just won the UEFA Cup. She was twenty-three.

They had met on the waltzers at St Leger Fair in

Doncaster when she was sixteen and a miner's daughter. He told her that he worked in a steelworks as saying 'I was a footballer would have sounded too flash, even though I was an unknown playing for a small club.' At the time he was with Scunthorpe United, then in the Fourth Division.

Kevin and his mate Phil Niles, a trainee teacher, offered Jean and her friend Wendy Devlin a lift home in Keegan's Ford Cortina. He told the girls that the car belonged to his dad, again, fearing that if he said it was his he would sound too flash. Although they accepted a lift, they jumped out at traffic lights in the centre of Doncaster.

'A few weeks later we bumped into Jean with another girl at the Top Rank ballroom in Doncaster and asked why she and Wendy had jumped out of the car,' he said in his autobiography. 'To me it showed that they were nice girls who had a bit of class. Phil quite liked Jean and I liked her mate, and we weren't sure who was going out with whom until I went to watch Jean in a school play and asked her afterwards if she would rather go out with Phil. She was happy with me and our relationship started from there.'

Jean was still doing her A-levels and he would pick her up from school. She only discovered that he was a footballer when he couldn't go with her to an ice-skating rink on a Saturday.

'Although she was a fully paid-up member of the

George Best Fan Club she was not impressed,' he said. 'I was a world away from Georgie Best. It was only after I had appeared on Match of the Day that people began to recognise me, and when it happened, it came as a big surprise after years of anonymity.'

In 1971, he transferred to Liverpool for £33,000. At the time of his wedding he was earning £100 a week. He celebrated by splashing out on a £2,000 Datsun. The wedding itself was a low-key affair. No *Hello!*-style coverage. No celebrity guests. No fanfares and no fans. Indeed, the ceremony was a spur-of-the-moment affair.

'Jean and I hadn't planned to get married for months, but I had a five-week ban for fighting with Billy Bremner and, as they say, every cloud has a silver lining, so we decided to use the time to get married quietly,' he said.

While Keegan went on to have a high-profile career in football—both as a player and manager—as well as appearing on TV and releasing records, Jean and their two daughters Laura and Sarah managed to stay out of the celebrity magazines.

4
Wag War One

Graeme Souness had already been capped for Scotland and captain of Liverpool, transferring there for a record £350,000 in 1978, when he met twenty-year-old Danielle Wilson, who had been dragged along to the match by a friend. She was a multi-millionaire's daughter who was not interested in his money unlike many other girls he met.

'She was a very rich girl with a very rich Daddy. She had a pampered lifestyle. But what Souness had was glamour. I would imagine that, given the type of woman she is, she would have been attracted to that,' said a friend.

Danielle had already been divorced once and had an eighteen-month-old daughter. The couple got engaged after six months and were married two years later. Though no fan of the game, she said: 'He is a winner and I like that.'

At the wedding, she wore a straight, high-neck white dress, with dainty flowers in her long blonde hair.

He wore a white double-breasted suit with rose corsage.

By then, Souness was earning £80,000 a year at Liverpool, but after they were wed he moved to Sampdoria in Italy on a two-year contract, earning £650,000. Souness adopted Danielle's daughter Chantelle and the couple had two children of their own—Frazer and Jordan. Meanwhile he developed a taste for vintage champagne, designer clothes, gleaming Daimlers and liberally doused himself with aftershave.

But Danielle did not relish being a WAG. She walked out on their marriage after eight years after issuing an ultimatum—your family or football. He chose football.

'Money can't buy you happiness,' she said. 'It was his obsession with football that killed our relationship.'

On another occasion she complained: 'On the rare occasions he took me out he talked about nothing but football.' She wanted to get to know the man behind the footballer.

At the time he had moved to Rangers as player-manager and was dedicated to making them Europe's top club, while she comforted herself with her father's £40 million fortune. That year, Rangers won the Scottish Football League, the first of nine consecutive victories which took them into the UEFA Champions League.

'If you want to be successful you have to make sacrifices,' he said. 'I have sacrificed a great deal this year and I don't think I have ever wanted anything in football so much as this title.'

Nevertheless, when he left Rangers in 1991, he said he wanted to spend more time with his children who were living with his estranged wife near London. She did not want to live in Scotland and spent much of her time in Majorca. Even during the football season, he travelled back and forth to see his two sons and adopted daughter.

In fact, he had wanted to stay on at Rangers, saying: 'Everybody has to make sacrifices at some stage in their life. I have had to make a very important one in mine, but that is the measure of my commitment to this club.'

Even so he refused to take off the gold crucifix he wore around his neck. It had been given to him by Danielle, who was a Catholic. Rangers was a traditionally Protestant team.

Alex Ferguson, who had managed him in the Scottish national team was sympathetic. He said he was sorry to hear about the break-up and Souness thanked him for his understanding. Then Fergie commented: 'Well, ye'll no' be gettin' yer rations tonight then Graeme, eh?'

Souness returned to Liverpool as manager saying, perhaps stretching a point: 'My family comes first.'

Indeed, Danielle made a great issue of the amicability of their parting, pointing to the long weekends they spent all together as a family, saying: 'Neither of us

wants to marry anyone else, so why bother divorcing?'
But divorce they did.

When he underwent a heart-bypass operation in
1992, he had a new WAG, Karen Levy—a blonde who
had been a contestant in Miss UK and a Bond girl—at
his bedside. Four years younger than Danielle, she had
formerly been a host of *Sale of the Century*. They had
only met five weeks earlier. Danielle said that his decision to have his new girlfriend with him did not sit well
with their children.

'I'm hoping they will get over it in time but I can tell
they're both still upset,' she said.

After surgery Souness took a holiday in Arizona
with Karen to recuperate—and suffered something of
an emotional breakdown.

'Karen would try to get up early and sneak out of
the room for a gym work-out,' he recalled. 'She didn't
want me to feel bad about her being able to exercise
vigorously while I was still trying to regain my strength.
But I would open my eyes, realise she'd gone and lose
control of my feelings. This would go on for an hour
on a daily basis. By the time you work out what's going
on it's even more hurtful.

'What's happening is that the surgery has left you
feeling less of a man. Not the macho Graeme Souness.
When I asked the medical people for their opinion they
told me it was a natural and commonplace reaction to
what I'd been through.'

Karen and Graeme.

Image-conscious Souness had spent £4,000 on a nose job and £35,000 on a bathroom in his luxury Tudor-style home in Mere, Cheshire. The taps alone cost £1,000 each and another £25,000 was spent on doing up the guest bathrooms.

Karen had her own mock-Tudor mansion in Cheadle, Greater Manchester, where she lived with her two children from a previous marriage. Readying herself for a WAG lifestyle, Karen took her ex-husband, wealthy fashion wholesaler Jonathan Levy to court over money.

Souness was in Manchester Crown Court with her for the hearing when he should have flown out to Cyprus for a European Cup Winners' Cup match in Limassol. She dressed in black and told the press: 'I have nothing to say.'

They were later chided by Liverpool supporters when they were pictured kissing on the front page of the *Sun* under the headline 'Lover-pool'. It appeared on the day the third anniversary of the Hillsborough disaster, where ninety-six fans died as a result of mistakes made by officials, and which the police tried to cover up by blaming the fans for the deaths. Souness was censured by the club's board and later said he regretted having sold the story of his heart operation to the *Sun* (which is hated on Merseyside for wrongly attacking Liverpool fans after the disaster).

Danielle then broke her silence to accuse her former husband of hard-hearted behaviour to her and their sons in an explosive interview for which she was paid £20,000 pound but which cost the Mirror Group £750,000 in damages . She told the *People* that in November 1992 Souness had ordered her and their children to leave their £500,000 farmhouse home in Worplesdon, Surrey, by Christmas Eve and he forced to her sign a 'bizarre no men in the house' contract while she still lived there.

'He couldn't wait to get us out,' said Danielle. 'He asked: 'When are you going, next week?' He sent us an eviction notice telling us to get out by Christmas Eve. I don't know where we were meant to go for Christmas.

'When I asked him why he had sent it, he said: 'I don't give a bugger. Go on, get out and take the children with you.' As far as I was concerned he could have the house back—even though it was meant to be a gift to the children and was going to be held in trust for them. After all that was what really mattered to him, not the children.'

Danielle said she had turned the house into a heaven for Frazer, Jason and her daughter by a previous marriage, Chantelle, then eighteen.

'I will never forget that day,' said Danielle. 'He talked about the heart by-pass operation he'd had earlier in the year and said he wanted to live his own life because he had no idea how long he had. We were not part of it and I just felt as if I was an unpaid housekeeper. I was fed up with him dictating who I could and couldn't have in the house. I lived there with his children. It was their home which he'd promised them. But he treated me as if I was a tenant even though I am still his wife and they are still his children.'

Souness's response to these serious accusations the newspaper reported was immediate. 'Criticism is part and parcel of my business but I can never accept this— I've been accused of something which is just a load of lies from start to finish.' He sued Danielle for libel.

Another complaint was that Souness had publicly humiliated her by allowing a national newspaper to picture him with Karen at his hospital bedside while he recovered from the by-pass op. Danielle then said she did not have a bad word to say about Souness, but the report caused a family rift as tearful Frazer refused to visit his father in hospital.

Still Danielle said she had nothing but praise for the man who was battling to get fit again and she was delighted when Frazer later made up with his dad. Though while they were still married, she confide to the paper, her feelings were more mixed.

'With him being obsessed with his job, I felt we were more possessions rather than I was his wife and they were his children,' she said. 'I wanted a family and a husband who was supportive and he just wanted his job. We were an adornment, like something you put on the mantlepiece—another trophy to be displayed for a while, then left to gather dust.'

Family life first began to crumble when Souness became boss of Glasgow Rangers in 1986, she claimed.

'Graeme has always been the type of person who when his team loses it affects him badly and being the closest people to him at the time, the whole family suffered. He had mood swings. He was either up or down and very difficult to live with.'

When Souness was offered a second contract by

Rangers—which he accepted without consulting her—Danielle realised football would always be first love and she left him. This was the downside of being a WAG.

'It was his temperament which was more to blame because he would never accept defeat,' she said about his mood at the time. 'And in that first year at Rangers he wasn't very successful so he basically took it out on us. It was three months into the new season and I said to him: 'Either you change or we go.' His reply was: 'I give 100 per cent to my job so you go.' That was that.'

Speaking of his two seasons as Liverpool manager, she said: 'He is finding it very hard to come to terms with the fact that the team hasn't done well. He said to me on several occasions that he didn't realise the Liverpool job was going to be as difficult as it turned out to be. Graeme is not a loser—he will never stay where he loses.

But his new WAG Karen professed to see Souness very differently when they were introduced in a Cheshire wine bar, soon after she had left her first husband Jonathan. Souness told the tale that he had seen her photograph in a magazine shortly before he met her and their meeting had been blind date arranged by Manchester City's Mike Summerbee with another pal that did not quite come off. Nevertheless, there was an instant rapport.

'He was so funny, so charming,' Karen said. 'That night was the first time I'd smiled in fifteen months and

I haven't stopped smiling since. He may be strong but he is a total gentleman, kind, considerate and affectionate. He is full of the type of mischief that makes you want to throw your arms around him.'

He, too, was immediately smitten.

'Very soon we realised we were in love,' he said. 'Soon we were even talking about marriage. Our love grew very quickly.'

Within a month, the thirty-three-year-old mother of two was keeping vigil by his hospital bed.

'His heart problem came as a tremendous shock, but it drew us even closer together,' she said. 'It made me feel very protective.'

At the time, he felt it was touch and go.

'I did feel at one point that I wasn't sure whether I was ever going to come out of that place,' he said. 'I thought I was going to die.'

In 1994, they married in a secret ten-minute ceremony in a Las Vegas hotel, attended by her parents.

'This is one of the greatest days of my life—I couldn't be happier,' said Souness.

Graeme's brother Gordon said: 'I'm very happy for them. As long as Graeme is happy, so am I. They are an ideal couple. They have kept the wedding quiet.'

During the vows, the couple pledged their love to her two children, Daniel and Lauren, giving them special certificates. Later they had a son of their own named James.

Meanwhile, a legal battle with his former wife Danielle erupted. In the High Court in London, Danielle asked for more than £500,000 on top of maintenance and school fees because she claimed her husband had put 'undue pressure' on her to make an agreement. In response, Souness's lawyers countered with a breach of a court order to give full details of her bank accounts. He wanted to know where £1.8 million from a Spanish account under Danielle's control had gone.

The *Sunday Times* reported that while Danielle had a sports car, a luxury villa in Spain and a four-bedroom house in the Cheshire stockbroker belt, she was on legal aid. Legal fees were expected to run into tens of thousands of pounds.

Under the original agreement, he was to give her £500,000 plus valuable land in Spain, along with £10,000 in maintenance and school fees for their two sons. However, she had the money to buy a £145,000 property in Bramhall, Cheshire, when she moved back to England in 1994. Her villa in Majorca, surrounded by pine trees and overlooking Palma Bay, was on the market for £1.25 million.

The *Sunday Times* reported she left for a shopping trip in her £25,000 red Z28 Chevrolet Camero. But she pointed out they misunderstood.

'Everything I've got is in the villa. It could sell for £800,000 but my brother has £300,000 invested in it,' she said in response. Her previous car had belonged to her brother and the new one had been imported from Florida by her mother.

'I did not have a car so she loaned it until I got the money and things sorted out,' she said.

Her solicitor Karen Barham said: 'The reason the legal aid board will not include the Spanish property is because it is a property which is a subject matter of the dispute. She is a non-working mother and has no income of her own.'

The property in Cheshire had been bought by Danielle's father, shopping tycoon Austin Wilson, who lived in Majorca. 'She remains liable to repay him,' added Barham.

But Souness's solicitor Gerard Cukier offered that the villa was not an issue in the proceedings: 'Danielle Souness built the villa on land which was part of the divorce settlement and there is no dispute over it.'

Soon after, Souness was back in court suing Mirror Group Newspapers for the interview with Danielle the *People* had published. While saying he was 'extremely happy' with his new wife Karen, the story and the resulting court case had put an enormous strain on their relationship. He squeezed her hand as the allegations of meanness were read out in court.

While Karen joined Danielle's gaze across the courtroom, Souness avoided looking at his first wife. The two women were engaged in a fashion battle with

Karen turning up to court in a chic above-the-knee lemon suit while Danielle looked stunning in a black suit, reminiscent of the power-dressing style of the 1980s, as she put her best designer-shod foot forward and striding into court to face her former husband.

'Worse, she's also had to bear the inevitable comparison with his new wife Karen,' the *Sunday Mirror* pitched in. 'The age gap is only four years—Danielle is 39, Karen 35—but it seems so much more, probably because Danielle has spent the last few years struggling to bring-up two sons on her own. Karen's daily routine can hardly be more taxing than juggling visits to the gym, beautician and hairdresser.

'Still, Danielle has turned up each day, impeccably turned-out in an expensive suit. Then Karen has appeared in a more expensive suit, a couple of sizes smaller. When the younger model your ex dumped you for is a one-time Bond Girl, life really is a bitch.'

Even the upmarket *Sunday Times* could not resist taking a pop at 'hardman Souness' and his 'leggy lovers' under the headline: 'It's all blonde ambition—home or away.'

The court battle drew on. 'Day after day, they were pictured leaving the court hand-in-hand. She edged out smiles for the cameras focussed on her perfectly-coiffed hair and short skirts which showed off her lithe, fit figure. Souness, fashionably attired in suit and tie, kept a straight face throughout.'

The newspaper unkindly pointed out that the resemblance between Karen and Danielle was uncanny, quoting a friend saying: 'His new wife seems to be a clone of the old wife.' Then the paper asked: 'So what does it take to be a Souness wife, to be a match for the type of man who reportedly used an American Express gold card, instead of the traditional 10-pence coin, for a pre-match toss-up?'

The *Sunday Times* decided that Karen was arguably more naturally beautiful and quoted a tabloid identifying his wives as the 'Two main players kitted out for court'. Souness himself was a fashion fanatic: 'It really got to Souness when his hair started to thin, it really cut him up.' Men like Souness wanted to look good and they liked their women to follow suit.

'But the life of a footballer's wife is not all glamour. They live the high life: superb homes, clothes, trips. Their children want for little. But in return, they give up any hope of privacy,' the *Sunday Times* said. 'Then, there are the constant moves. At any moment you can be told you are being transferred. You live a nomadic lifestyle and that must be unsettling. The wives are having to build up new relationships time after time. They also know their husbands are very attractive to other women, they are always on the telly and in the paper. They know women are throwing themselves at them, because they used to do it themselves.'

The newspaper said that footballers generally did

not have the best reputation as husbands and asked: 'So why do women flock to the altar with them?'

Bill McMurdo, one of Scotland's top football agents, said: 'I think it's the power; the players are glorified. It's the nearest they are going to come to a celebrity. You don't have too many Frank Sinatras running about in Glasgow.' But he cautioned: 'It's not all glamorous. Every up has a down.'

Back in court, Souness wept when he talked about his love of his children. He told the jury: 'Because of the job I had, I experienced great emotional highs. When you have a child that eclipses everything else, and I think I am like most fathers. They are the most important thing on this planet, along with my [current] wife.'

He said he was only a telephone call away from his ex-wife who only had to ask and he would give for the children. Then, when he first saw the article in his local newsagent headlined: 'You're a Dirty Rat, Souness,' he felt numb.

His counsel Lord Williams said: 'He is devoted to these children. He dotes on them. Apart from his present wife Karen Souness, they are the most important thing in his life. Judas betrayed Jesus Christ for thirty pieces of silver. Danielle Souness did it for the £15,000 she was paid for the article.'

Under a £1-million Scottish divorce 'clean break' cash settlement, he said Souness gave her £560,000 in cash and land in Majorca worth £500,000. He also agreed to pay private school fees for the children and provided a £1-million home for them in Surrey. His ex-wife was supposed to provide £100,000 towards the house, he alleged, but never did.

Souness also asked her to pay £100 a month rent. She offered £1 a month and they never reached an agreement. He did serve her with a notice to quit but never enforced it and he never turned them out. She left with the children to live in Majorca in February 1993.

As to the 'no men in the house' contract, Lord Williams said it was an agreement that if she re-married, her new husband would not live in the house and she would not move another man in. Then there was the allegation that he refused to pay the children's school fees. He said he agreed to pay all school fees while they were in England, only stopping when she took the children to live in Majorca.

Souness said he didn't think Majorca was the place for his children. His younger son Jordan, then ten, had been having learning difficulties and his teachers wanted him to see a psychologist. Evidence was later introduced that Jordan was frightened of going to Majorca and hated school there. The story that Souness was 'tight-fisted' when it came to his children was 'vicious, savage and untrue,' Lord Williams said and the jury should award him 'massive' damages.

It was quite untrue that she had to grovel to him for

cash. Souness also found the claim by his ex-wife in the newspaper that 'he doesn't give a monkey's because he knows my father will help his grandchildren' to be 'a deeply offensive and wicked remark'. Souness bought Danielle and the children the £1-million mansion, Norton Farm in Worplesdon, Surrey, and spent £250,000 doing it up.

Giving evidence, he said his ex-wife didn't like Scotland because it was 'too cold and wet'. Danielle moved to Majorca and he regularly flew out to see her and the family for five years before they finally parted.

'She was happy living in Majorca,' he said. 'Her ideal was for me to go there and do nothing. But I had always wanted to work. That was the way I had been brought up.'

Being an ex-WAG was not without risks. Defence counsel George Carman QC said: 'For the last five months you have had an application outstanding to have the mother of your children committed to prison.'

Souness told the High Court: 'The order was applied for on the advice of my lawyers. She has consistently not answered the questionnaire for more than two-and-a-half years.'

He said he had had no idea when the children were taken to live in Majorca.

'She did not tell me she was going to Majorca. When I phoned, I got a stranger on the telephone who told me she was lodging there with another female friend. They had come home to find the place empty. There was no furniture, just a fridge.'

He claimed that Danielle told the kids not to say anything to him about the move to Majorca in 1993, adding: 'Jordan did not even get the chance to say goodbye to his pals.'

Asked by Lord Williams what effect the newspaper story had had on him, Souness replied: 'Profound. There is not a day goes by when I do not think about it. It has been unbearable. Without a shadow of a doubt, it has had an effect on those people close to me. The most damaging thing of all is that my two sons have been affected.'

He also told the court that his eldest son Frazer, then fourteen had vowed never to speak to him again because of his new love Karen Levy, now his wife. The bust-up happened when Souness phoned his family from hospital, two days before he had heart bypass surgery. However, they had since made up.

George Carman QC, defending the Mirror Group, then asked Souness about his earnings. He replied that they included in the region of £600,000 to £650,000 during a two-year spell in Italy, a £2.2-million share deal while he was player-manager of Glasgow Rangers, and a £200,000 signing-on fee when he joined Liverpool as manager. He was recently given a £300,000 contract to manage Turkish side Galatasaray. Souness denied telling his ex-wife he was worth £8 million.

He went on to tell the court of his love for Karen.

'We met in March 1992. Within one month I knew I wanted to spend my life with her,' he said.

Carman told the court Souness made a fortune from football. When he joined Italian side Sampdoria in 1984, he got a signing on fee of £350,000. He earned almost £3 million in his time at Rangers, including a £2.2 million share deal. He also got two interest-free loans totalling £245,000, including one of £125,000 for work on his house in Edinburgh.

When asked how he felt when he served an eviction order on Danielle in November 1992, days after moving into a £1 million house with Karen, Souness said: 'I'm not proud of it but I had been reasonable for nearly two years. It was the only option left open to me.'

The *People* said he gave her twenty-eight days to quit the Surrey farmhouse. Souness says that deadline was never enforced.

He reportedly looked drained and emotional as he told the court: 'My wife has developed an incredible appetite for telling lies ever since I met my new wife, and that's why I'm here.'

He admitted showing his sons the story because he felt his eldest boy had to see what his mother had done.

'I didn't want to be here today,' he said. 'I just want to prove what was said was all lies.'

Asked if he sought to 'dominate and control' Danielle, he said: 'A Bengal tiger could not do that to my ex-wife.'

Mr Carmen said Danielle was desperate when he refused to give her money for the children.

'She has never been desperate from the day she was born to today,' said Souness, pointing out that, after her £1-million divorce settlement, Danielle was a wealthy woman in her own right.

Souness defended his behaviour on the grounds that he had worked hard for everything he had. Mr Carman said: 'Probably most people in this courtroom have had to work for what they have got.' Souness looked towards his ex-wife—sitting, wearing a black suit, in the front row a few feet away—and said: 'I can point to one person that's not, sir.'

He was then asked how he had met Karen, who was also wearing black that day.

'I met her in March 1992 in a wine bar in Manchester,' he said. 'That put a totally different complexion on my life. It's the best thing that ever happened to me. It changed me as a man. It made me the happiest man on this planet.'

There was an angry flare-up when Mr Carman referred to Karen becoming the footballer's 'mistress'.

'I don't like you using that word,' said Souness.

'Lover—would you prefer that?' asked Carman.

'Yes, I would,' said Souness.

Carman continued: 'She became your lover and cohabited with you before marriage—there's nothing wrong with it.'

'We were in love, yes,' said Souness.

Taking the stand, Danielle said that Souness's job as manager of Rangers put a strain on the relationship.

'He disappeared for two days—and at the time it was my birthday,' she said. 'There were arguments—we were going through a very, very rough patch. I felt he tried to vent his feelings on me. By the end of 1988 I felt so low about myself. I had lost all my confidence…

'He made derogatory remarks about everything I did. I lost my own respect for myself. I told him something had got to change. He said he was putting a hundred per cent into his job. I took that to mean I was not in his future and that was that. That was the push to go. That was the end.'

It then came out that Danielle had won a race to seize £565,000 in a joint account in Majorca. Souness and his lawyer had flown 850 miles out to the Spanish island to grab the cash before she could claim it. But they arrived at the bank five minutes too late, bumping into Danielle's father—who she had asked to safeguard the half million for her—on the way out after switching the money into another account. Souness's counsel, Lord Williams, accused her of acting 'like a thief in the night'.

She said that she sold the story about the collapse of their marriage to the *People* because 'I thought I had the right to tell my side'. Lord Williams accused her of betraying her youngest son Jordan by revealing details of his dyslexia.

'To sell a private matter about that young boy and his problem to a newspaper was a betrayal by a mother,' he said.

The jury vindicated Souness's account and awarded him £750,000 in damages and stuck Mirror Group Newspapers with an estimated £250,000 in costs. As he walked out of the High Court arm in arm with the new WAG, Karen, Souness said: 'I am delighted that I have been vindicated. It has been an enormous strain both for me and my wife. I just want to go home and get on with my life.' In the end, Souness accepted £100,000 provided MGN dropped their threatened appeal.

'My sole purpose has always been to clear my name,' he said.

Further the allegations that he had taken bungs were 'totally false,' he insisted, and the subject of further libel actions. In 1996, Souness won another £100,000 from the *Mail on Sunday* who made disparaging claims about Souness's behaviour.

5
Wags Are Go

The courtroom battle of WAGs was won by Karen, according to sports journalist Shelley Webb (herself married to footballer Neil Webb) writing in the *Sunday Times*. She said that Danielle was built along the same lines as the first Mrs Best, Angie, who 'became an icon of bosomy, big-haired good looks'.

'Both Danielle and Angie shared an almost fetishistic passion for grandiose external adornment. You could always tell a player's wife: lots of jewellery, more make-up and no conversation.'

Webb then compared Karen to Best's second wife Alex Pursey who had married George Best without a highlight or white shoe in sight. She enjoyed lacrosse, swam for Surrey, had eight GCSEs and a business-studies qualification, and was a late starter in the nightclubbing stakes. With Karen Levy a new types of WAGs were popping everywhere.

'Footballers' wives are not even supposed to be able to spell lacrosse. Or if we can, we think it's some sort of casserole dish,' Shelley said.

Assessing Karen, she said: 'Yes, she is blonde. Yes, she is beautiful. But what marked her out above all was a sober, sophisticated, expensively suited elegance not hitherto associated with soccer wifedom. Let's not beat about the bush: the new Karen Levy, a former Bond girl, exudes class from every pore. The perfectly glosssed lips spoke volumes about the care which she had taken for her appearance in court. Danielle Souness suffered immensely from the comparison.'

Shelley noted that WAGgery itself had changed since the days of Angie Best. *Cosmopolitan* was writing about football. The new breed of WAGs were no longer a mere appendage. They were becoming a force to be reckoned with—literally. Claire Ince, wife of England international Paul, had attracted the attention of the Italian press during her husband's recent transfer from Manchester United to Inter. They said Claire 'wore the trousers' in the Ince household after she allegedly rejected a series of lakeside homes.

Isabelle Cantona was another WAG who happily stayed out of the limelight. She had her own career as a language teacher and her own views on life, which she has no hesitation in airing. She was, reportedly, behind Eric's decision to leave Manchester United.

'One of the best examples of the new breed is Karren Brady, married to Stoke City's Paul Peschisolido,' Shelley said. 'They met at Birmingham City, where he was a player and she was and is managing director. She has not only been responsible with owner David Sullivan and manager Barry Fry for restoring the fortunes of the club, but has her own cable television show, the *Brady Bunch*. She is certainly a career girl, yet is not above posing in a pair of silky football shorts.'

Then there was Ruth Gordon, the twenty-seven-year-old fiancée of Liverpool defender John Scales. She did a stint as a Page 3 girl—'football's equivalent of the casting couch'—but her interests include painting, architecture and the novels of F. Scott Fitzgerald.

'It's the archetypal stereotype,' Ruth said. 'Footballer and Page 3 girl. So, when somebody asks me the inevitable questions ("Why do you take your clothes off?" "Did you meet in Stringfellows?"), I invariably reply, "I can't possibly answer that, you can't expect me to have brains as well."'

Back in the day, Shelley said, WAGs only had to know the quickest way to the shops, what colour tights to wear with white shoes and how much Malibu they could drink without getting hiccups.

But fashions had changed. Out were the bottom-skimming dresses and tight sparkly tops that were more boob than tube, the white stilettos, the fake orange tan and the big hair. In came a more understated, classic designer look, of the sort that suits Rachel Platt, wife of the then England captain. It seemed that, with more British footballers playing in Europe, European chic was rubbing off on the WAGs too.

Those donning the new designer look included Samantha Jane, the bride of the Blackburn Rovers striker Chris Sutton, Michelle Lineker, Leslie Ash, wife of Ipswich striker Lee Chapman, and Jill Hughes, who was married to Chelsea's new signing, Mark Hughes.

Suzy Barnes, wife of John Barnes, the Liverpool and England midfielder, said: 'Many wives have always been stylish. They have had to be. A footballer earning large sums of money has always been seen as a good catch.'

But she complained it was not an easy life.

'You are surrounded by fans, pictures are being taken of you and you are very much on view,' said Suzy. 'When it first happened, it terrified me and I still can't get used to being recognised. But now I get fan mail telling me how beautiful my children are or how much they like an outfit I wore.'

But what about me? Shelley Webb asked in conclusion: 'I've never won a prize for elegance, what with my bitten-down nails and midfielder's legs, but I do have a first-class honours degree in English and history. Perhaps my time has come. Malibu, anyone?'

With the court case behind them, the battle of the Souness ex-WAG and new-WAG finally reached an uneasy truce in 1999 when Graeme, Danielle and a very pregnant Karen turned up at the wedding of his adopted daughter Chantelle in Majorca.

The *Daily Record* said that Souness and his ex were

'not exactly lovey dovey, but they put the brakes on any outward show of hostility'. The bruising court case seemed to have finally aired out all the dirty laundry that had been left.

But hostility did come to the surface when Scotland's hardman visited the Wilmslow home of Karen's ex Jonathan Levy apparently to discuss Levy's parental responsibilities towards twenty-year-old Daniel, Souness's stepson, who had been busted for drink-driving. After a dust-up, Souness emerged with his right arm in plaster.

Souness, then manager of Blackburn Rovers, said he hurt himself while acting during self-defence in the fracas. Levy, who sustained head and facial injuries in the tussle, told police he had been assaulted.

'I can confirm that, during discussions with my stepson's father about the discharge of his parental responsibilities, an incident took place in which I suffered a hand injury while defending myself,' said Souness in a statement which he said he had issued to 'avoid unnecessary speculation'.

The police arrested Souness and bailed him pending further enquiries. In the end, no charges were brought.

In 2014, he and Karen celebrated their twentieth wedding anniversary in the Caribbean.

'I'd like to think that these days I'm a better husband, a better dad, just a better person to be around,' he said. A reformed man, he had even become an arm-chair critic as a pundit with Sky Sports.

6
A Wag in the Family

Paul Gascoigne was seen as the most talented footballer of his generation. He achieved fame at the 1990 FIFA World Cup when he cried after receiving a yellow card in the semi-final with West Germany which meant he would have been suspended for the final had England won the game. While he was at Newcastle United, he was described by chairman Stan Seymour as 'George Best without the brains'. Nor did he have the good looks while details of his love life did not surface in the press until he transferred to Italian team Lazio in 1992.

That August, the *Sunday Mirror* reported that twenty-five-year-old mother-of-two and former model Sheryl Kyle was setting up home with him in Italy—under the headline 'Sexy Sheryl jets in to share love nest with soccer hero'.

They stayed together in a hotel in Rome, while arrangements were made for them to share a luxury villa. A friend said: 'They have missed each other madly since Paul went to Italy and have been on the phone to each other constantly.'

Sheryl had separated from her estate agent husband Colin a year earlier and said at first that she and Gazza were 'just good friends'. Then she admitted that they were 'very close' and the Geordie joker was 'loving and gentle'. She flew to Rome with her two-year-old son Mason. Her six-year-old daughter Bianca remained at home in England with relatives. She joined them later as a full WAG.

Shelley and Gazza.

Gazza's new bosses at Lazio were delighted, believing that Sheryl could tame his hell-raising. He had been ordered to cut down on beer after he arrived there a month earlier a stone overweight and his high jinks had kept his bodyguards constantly on their toes. His favourite trick was to send them into a panic by 'vanishing'—only to emerge later from inside a cupboard.

Before he left for Italy, Gazza regularly stayed at Sheryl's £250,000 home in Hoddesdon, Hertfordshire. She said then: 'He loves my kids and they adore him.'

Friends feared that the romance might fizzle out if Sheryl stayed in England. They had already fallen out while they spent £20,000 holidaying together at Florida's Disney World. She blew her top when he frolicked with his Geordie friends. But the *Mirror* reported they were now more committed than ever. The relationship seemed to be working as he relished playing dad to Mason.

'We always heard Gazza had a wild reputation,' said Emilio Parisi, barman in Rome's Hilton Hotel. 'But he spends most of his time with his "family" by the pool.'

Gazza's drinking buddy, 'Five Bellies' Gardener, said to have been paid £3,000 a month to keep him company in Rome, had also turned his back on *la dolce vita* for the love of his girlfriend Joanne Gibson, another blonde, and their two-year-old son Liam.

Soon Gazza had trimmed down and was match fit. Lazio's bosses intuition about Sheryl's influence seemed to have been on the money. Then 'Five Bellies' was sent home after clashing with Gazza's younger brother Carl. He was charged with assaulting Joanne, though she dropped the charges in court. Gazza and Sheryl also flew home for the wedding of his actress sister Anna-Maria where Gazza was best man.

Gazza was soon in trouble with Lazio again. After missing a match ostensibly due to a bout of 'flu, he flew off to Euro Disney with Sheryl and the kids. For Christmas he bought her a £30,000 red Toyota Celica, but she put her foot down and banned him from driving it. He had to buy another for himself.

Under the influence of his new WAG, he had also given up his shell suits, treating himself to £10,000-worth of suits and shoes from Armani and Versace. He bought Sheryl a £20,000 bracelet and another £30,000 was spent on designer clothes from a string of Rome boutiques. But while they were back in England for Christmas, their villa in Rome was burgled. More trouble ensued after they returned to Italy when her five-bedroom Hertfordshire home, complete with lavishly equipped white kitchen, huge bathroom, Italian marble fireplace and lakeside view, was repossessed by the mortgage company. Her husband Colin said: 'The house was repossessed after I was made bankrupt last year. I moved out some time ago, but Sheryl continued to live there.'

There were other troubles, too. When his boozy

Geordie pals turned up for the big match between Lazio and Sampdoria, Sheryl quit their villa and headed for home. Sheryl's closest friend and former neighbour Wendy Clarke said: 'She hasn't split up from Paul but she has no plans to return to Rome at the moment. I can't tell you any more than that.'

A close friend of Gazza said: 'They have been having a very tough time and it wouldn't surprise me in the least if they have split up. Sheryl is very aloof. Gazza's family haven't warmed to her at all and she hates his drinking buddies like Jimmy "Five Bellies" Gardner. Her kids adore Paul. They call him Dad and he loved being the family man. But it's been a rough ride between the couple since they moved to Rome.'

She was also concerned after Gazza had been fined £9,000 by Lazio for belching into a reporter's microphone. While Gazza poured out his heart to Lazio president Sergio Cragnotti, Sheryl fought back the tears as she said she could not bear the lonely life of a 'soccer widow' in Rome while holed up in Gazza's £250,000 home in Dobbs Weir, Hertfordshire.

'I have nothing to say. Go away. Leave me alone,' the WAG told a reporter through the letterbox.

Her mother Mrs Cecilia Failes told of the pressures facing Sheryl in Rome. The ex-model felt bored, neglected and frustrated after £15,000-a-week Gazza made it clear to her who had the top billing at their home—'Football comes first.'

Their Italian sixteen-room villa with a swimming pool and manicured gardens cost Lazio £7,500 a month to rent. It was ringed by a seven-foot wall and surrounded by security cameras. But to her it was like a prison, despite its six acres of grounds. To a twenty-nine-year-old girl with a love of late nights and noisy clubs, it was purgatory. The presence of his beer-swilling mates did not help. Lots of lasagne washed down by a lake of lager was not her idea of a good time.

'Our test proves they're a perfect love match'.

Even sneaking out of the villa was an ordeal. While the kids were in school, she would make for the nearest shopping centre. But the Italian paparazzi kept tabs on her movements 24/7. Even going to the local hairdresser for a WAG essential, to have her roots bleached, became a nightmare.

Only rarely could she count on a night out with her man. Even then they had to run the gauntlet. Otherwise Gazza went out without her. On one occasion he was spotted dining with five friends at the exclusive restaurant Sabbatini's in Piazza Santa Maria. The bill came to £900 which, an eyewitness said, was 'mostly beer and wine'.

At midnight Gazza drove a tiny Fiat 500 round and round the fountain in the middle of the square outside the restaurant, bellowing loudly. But Gazza letting off steam was little comfort to Sheryl. In desperation she would phone her mum. In just two months she had clocked up a phone bill of nearly £2,000.

Mrs Failes admitted the couple's relationship had come under strain because of the professional pressure put on the £5.5-million Lazio star. She said: 'The Italians are football fanatics and Paul has to work, work, work. He trains twice a day, is often away from home staying in hotels and has to live and breathe football. I can understand why Sheryl decided to come home. There is more to life than just sitting about.'

And that's what Sheryl spent most of her time doing while the £750,000-a-year star trained and tried to earn his keep for Lazio. Nevertheless, her mum denied the couple were splitting up.

'They are still very much in love and Sheryl is already missing him a lot,' Mrs Failes said. 'She will see Paul shortly when he comes back to play for England at Wembley. And whatever their difficulties, I'm sure they will work it out.'

The children were missing Gazza, too.

'They look up to him as their own father and always call him 'daddy',' she said. 'He was wonderful with them.'

Gazza was said to have doted on Mason and Bianca and was hit hard when they left. He did everything possible to make their stay in a foreign country full of happiness, even making a surprise appearance at their school Christmas party near Rome and joining in the carols and nativity scenes. The parent of a child in Mason's class said: 'He and Sheryl seemed a perfect couple. They were very much together. It was a very happy family scene.'

But it had been a traumatic Christmas for Gazza. His father was ill, his career was halted by injury and his villa had been burgled. And there was press speculation about their relationship, which had often been a stormy one. Some said they were ill-suited. She had lived the yuppie lifestyle in up-market Hoddesdon, while he was a Geordie skinhead whose idea of the high life was six pints, a bag of chips and a Mars bar on Saturday night. But after Gazza fell for the alluring blonde, Sheryl clung on tight.

'We are a couple,' she said.

The friction had begun on a holiday in Florida the previous summer where Sheryl objected to Gazza's show-off antics on the beach. There were also rows between Sheryl and the soccer star's family who were with them. The holiday left its mark, but it was thought that Sheryl had put it all behind her when she travelled to Rome to start a new life with Gazza.

He spoke of his 'deep pain' at the breakup and took out his anger on her ex, Colin Kyle, who had also been speaking to the press.

'You have called my lass a slag,' he told thirty-year-old Colin over the phone. 'Let's sort this out man to man. No one calls my lass that—I want to meet you in a field.'

Kyle told the *Sunday Mirror*: 'He was calling me every name under the sun. I said I didn't care and that my children were my only concern. I told him I was recording the conversation and he slammed the phone down instantly. I'd gone round to Sheryl's house to talk about the kids but she tried to shut the door. I lost my temper and we screamed at each other. Two hours later, I had Gazza on the phone ranting and raving at me. That was when he wanted to fight me.'

But then a fight broke out between Colin and Sheryl and the police were called.

'I thought it wouldn't last between those two,' Colin said. 'I had heard they had been fighting like cat and dog. But I don't care about their relationship. Whatever brings my kids closer to me makes me happier. I'm fed up hearing about poor old Gazza. He doesn't seem to be getting on too well in Italy and now his girl has left.'

Speaking from the small house near Hertford he then shared with his new girlfriend, Kyle dished the dirt.

'What's been happening is so hurtful, I've just had enough,' he said. 'Sheryl's ambition must have been to marry Gazza. She is volatile but calculating. I don't know what will happen with her now. She has undergone a character change since I first knew her. She was all prim and proper then, with bobbed hairstyle and long skirts. Now it's all mini-skirts—she used to think people like that were a joke.'

Colin, whose divorce from Sheryl had been finalised a month earlier, told how she first met Gazza.

'We were in a restaurant in Hoddesdon when he walked in. He had just joined Tottenham,' Colin said. 'Sheryl, who'd had a few drinks, walked up to him and said: 'Hello, are you Paul Gascoigne?' He said, 'Why-aye lass,' and that was it. It was totally out of character for her. She isn't interested in football.'

Some time later, Sheryl told Colin she had seen Gazza in a wine bar and he had asked her for a date.

'She said Gazza had given her his telephone number,' Colin revealed. 'Maybe she was trying to make me jealous. I just thought: 'Big deal'. I moved out that month. It was a fading marriage and it was a relief to get out.'

The divorce came through in September 1991,

citing Sheryl's adultery with Gascoigne and saying that he found it 'intolerable' to live with her. She and Gazza insisted that their sexual relationship only began after the marriage was over.

Colin met the midfield star when he returned his children after an access visit.

'Sheryl and I had rowed because she had phoned me to say, 'Keep the kids, I'm going out, don't bring them home.' I said, 'You had better be in, don't treat the kids like that.' A few minutes later, the phone rang and a voice said, 'It's Gazza. Bring the kids around and I will be there.'

'I went round and he opened the door. I said hello and he stood at the door looking down at me. He was in my house with my wife and he didn't even have the respect to acknowledge me. He said nothing at all.'

As the rift deepened between the Kyles, Gazza became involved in a tug of love over the children.

Sheryl told Colin: 'You are not Mason's dad anymore. Paul is his dad now. Paul, Mason and I are a happy family. Mason calls Paul Daddy.'

In repost Colin said: 'Sheryl wouldn't let me know if she was going to Italy with Paul or not. I had no idea what was going to happen to the kids.'

'Bianca stayed with me for nearly three months. Then one day, I picked up the *Sunday Mirror* and saw pictures of Sheryl in Florida with Gazza. There was no sign of Mason,' he said. 'Sheryl eventually made it clear

Mason was going to Italy with her. Some weeks later it was sprung on me in the space of a day that she was going to take Bianca as well. I cried hysterically. There was nothing I could do.'

'I always acknowledged that she was the best person to look after them, but I do have to see my kids. It was arranged that I would be given an address to write to and a telephone number to ring so I could keep in touch. For weeks I rang but didn't get a reply. I never got through to them, it was heart-breaking.'

'The final straw was when I sent Mason and Bianca birthday presents in October and they were sent back to Britain by Parcel Force. I know Sheryl and Paul came back at Christmas with the children, but she never got in contact and I never even saw the kids at Christmas. All that concerns me is that, whoever Sheryl's partner is, they treat my kids nicely, which I think he does. But why they've been putting me through this I just don't know.'

Printing Colin's heart-breaking story, the *Sunday Mirror* said they tried to get Sheryl's side of the story, but she refused to come to the door of Gazza's home in Dobbs Weir, where she was staying after leaving Italy.

The following day, she dismissed talk of a split, saying: 'The stories aren't true. I am still with Paul.' But she refused to say whether she will be returning to Gazza's £2-million luxury villa on the outskirts of Rome. However, friends said they would not be surprised if she returned to Italy shortly as her children had settled into a private school and had come to regard twenty-five-year-old Gazza as 'daddy'.

Meanwhile, he was missing his new family and told colleagues: 'I'm hoping she'll come back soon.'

A week later, Sheryl flew to Rome in an eye-catching spotted miniskirt, saying: 'I'm going out to see Paul and I'm really looking forward to it. He has got some time off so we will be together. We will spend the day together and everything is fine.'

Just forty-eight hours later, she flew home again, nearly slipping flat on her face when her cowboy boots skidded on Heathrow's polished floors as she fled from the media.

The new split came after yet another of Gazza's flare-ups—this time with a group of over-enthusiastic Italian paparazzi who tried to snap him outside a Rome bar as he and Sheryl had lunch with three English photographers. After a lot of pushing and shoving between the two sets of snappers, a fuming Gazza leapt into his car with Sheryl and drove off at speed. The photographers ended up explaining their story to police while a tearful Sheryl headed for the airport after another furious row. He was left in Italy with his actress sister Anna-Maria for company.

Soon Gazza was seen flying back to London with Sheryl's son Mason. When he returned to Italy, he called Jimmy 'Five Bellies' Gardner to cheer him up.

Meanwhile, he was piling on the pounds. The bosses at Lazio were putting him under pressure and it was thought he could lose his England place.

'Paul is besotted with Sheryl,' said a friend. 'But there are a lot of problems in the relationship and Gazza can't think of anything else. It is affecting his game. Paul hates it when she goes to England and tends to binge when she is away.'

This cut no ice with Lazio president Sergio Cragnotti who insisted: 'He cannot allow his football to be taken over by personal problems.'

But Gazza had not lost it completely. He set about channelling his massive off-the-field earnings in Italy through a secret company set up on Malta. Already a millionaire by the age of twenty-three, he would pay little or no tax on those earnings, saving him an estimated £690,000 on his new football-boot contract alone. This allowed Sheryl to splash out another £135,000 on a new four-bedroom mock-Tudor detached house in Stanstead Abbots, Hertfordshire. He paid cash and, for an additional £10,000, got furniture and furnishings thrown in.

The developers said: 'He didn't have to deal with the transaction himself, it was done through his solicitor—and Sheryl took responsibility for everything.'

The house, it was said, was almost identical to house she had shared with her husband Colin before it was repossessed. It was also said that he had bought her tens of thousands of pounds of jewellery to set up her own shop.

Next time Gazza flew home, Sheryl picked him up at the airport, kissing him even though he was now wearing a goatee. A family court judge had ordered her to stay in England so that her ex-husband could have access to the children, but she went to court to have the injunction varied. The judge then ruled that she could take the children to Italy, but only for four weeks at a time.

The reconciliation came as a relief to Sergio Cragnotti who said that Lazio were determined to hold on to Gazza. A month later, Sheryl and Mason were seen in crowd for Lazio's match against Foggia.

Unfortunately, Gazza was not on form that day. One Lazio fan put the blame on his romantic life: 'He's been affected by his girlfriend. Sheryl's not being able to live with him in Rome, with all the consequent comings and goings. And whenever she does get here, he seems to play badly.'

Nevertheless, he turned out for England, damaging his cheekbone in a clash with Dutch skipper Jan Wouters. Soon after he was seen with Sheryl and the kids on the rides at Thorpe Park in Surrey.

'Gazza was smiling all over his face and clowning about a bit for all the people watching,' said another patron. 'But he, Sheryl and the kids looked like one big happy family.'

Then came the stab in the back. His personal assistant Jane Nottage was sacked and went to the press. She told the *Sunday Mirror* that Sheryl was behind her dismissal as she was trying to distance Gazza from his old friends. The relationship, Nottage said, was causing heartache within his own close-knit family and she feared his obsession with the girl he'd lavished thousands on could damage his career.

'Paul is a sweetie when he's on his own,' Jane said. 'And we'd all be happy if he met the woman of his dreams. I'm not saying Paul Gascoigne would be easy to live with, but he has such an open, generous character that he deserves better than this. I think he should look very carefully at his relationships and ask if he's really happy and has the stability to play football in the way we know he can.'

She characterised his love life as 'muddled and confusing'.

'He and Sheryl were fighting all the time,' she said. 'It was just like the Battle of Waterloo.'

'Last year on Sheryl's birthday Paul got me to book a table for them at her favourite restaurant, the Hassler Hotel, at the top of the Spanish Steps in Rome. I even got them to organise a birthday cake. Paul and Sheryl arrived, had a drink, had a row—then abandoned the dinner.'

'In the early days I used to spend time patching up their arguments. It's a shame it's come to this.'

Jane said that Sheryl's relationship with his family had got so bad that she insisted on sitting in a different section of Rome's vast Olympic stadium rather than sit near his mother, Carol. She also said that Sheryl had, in fact, missed the wedding of his sister Anna-Maria.

'It's pathetic,' Jane said. 'Paul's family are his rock, his stability. He needs them and old friends like Jimmy Gardner.'

'People may have criticised Jimmy, but he has always been totally loyal to Paul. In ten years' time Jimmy will still be around, but will Sheryl? Paul should be thinking of his future and of people who will care about him when he's not Paul Gascoigne, superstar.'

There were also his parents to consider.

'His mum Carol is certainly not the clingy type of mother who doesn't want her little boy to have a girl-friend,' Jane said. 'I know for a fact that she'd be delighted if he found someone who'd really make him happy and provide him with a family of his own.

'His dad has always been very important to him and had been a mate as well as a father. But now I wonder if that's still the case—he seems totally obsessed by this woman. She obviously has something he needs.'

In response, Sheryl pointed out that the relation-ship had started so well.

'We were confident it would work but neither of us realised how much he would be away,' she said. 'I felt so isolated and lonely. I began to feel like a soccer widow and I suppose it didn't help that I hate football.'

Sheryl said they had no marriage plans but added: 'I intend spending the rest of my life with Paul. He is the best thing that has happened to me.'

She was then commuting between her new £130,000 Hertfordshire home and Rome to see Gazza. Meanwhile Jane was remaining in Rome to handle commercial deals for his teammates.

'I have been told by Paul's business advisors that he has decided he can do without anyone in Rome,' Jane said. 'The whole situation is very strange, especially as Sheryl has always been very nice to my face.'

While being chaotic and erratic, Jane said Gazza was generous and caring.

'But unfortunately, when he's with Sheryl all the spontaneity goes,' she said. 'He gets uptight and nervy. It's really very sad. She's so funny about his relationships with family and friends. In fact, anyone or anything he shows affection for. Paul is always the first person to visit a sick child in hospital or comfort someone when they're upset, but he changes when he's with Sheryl.'

Jane was expecting some retaliation from Sheryl after speaking out.

'I'm sure Sheryl will come back at me and say Paul was always slagging me off, but I just wouldn't trust her motives,' said Jane. 'Sheryl's even admitted she hates football, which can't be very encouraging for Paul. It's like Placido Domingo's wife saying "Oh do shut up, Darling" every time he bursts into song. I'd say that was rather off-putting.'

Then there was the drain on his bank account.

'He's spending huge sums of money on Sheryl, tens of thousands of pounds on clothes and jewellery as well as a sports car and setting up her and the children in a new house in England. It'll be helicopters and private planes next. I just hope he doesn't throw it all away and stays close to his family and friends.'

The *Sunday Mirror* urged 'Give her the boot Gazza.'

When Gazza returned to England for a World Cup qualifier against Poland, the *Mirror* remarked that there wasn't a player in Italy who marked him tighter than Sheryl when she met him at the airport. Then just a few days after England's humiliating 2-0 defeat by Norway, Gazza was snapped drinking with a topless Sheryl topping up her tan at their villa in Rome.

'Blonde divorcee Sheryl, 29—wearing a smile and little else—preferred sipping from a glass as young Mason took a playful sip from a bottle like his "lager-than-life" dad,' said the *People*.

The photographer said: 'I wouldn't say Gazza was drunk but, as they say in Italy, he was certainly *allegro*. He offered the bottle of beer to the child as if it was the normal thing to do. Then he took over and supped the lot. Sheryl noticed it was empty and came out with a glass of booze to top him up.'

England manager Graham Taylor had already warned Gascoigne about 'refuelling' between matches, while Lazio asked him to switch to wine, which was more suitable for the Mediterranean climate.

Gazza, Sheryl and the kids then took off for a holiday in Miami where they took two luxurious rooms in the Grand Floridian Hotel with views over the lagoon and Magic Kingdom. This time, he dumped his Geordie friends and family and took Sheryl's parents instead. But the couple soon got involved in a series of rows, one of which ended with her dramatically flying back to Britain. Managers at Lazio and England were concerned that his performances on the field have been hampered by his personal problems.

To make things worse, Jane Nottage then published a biography *Paul Gascoigne: The Inside Story* that was serialised in the *Sunday Mirror*. In it, she revealed that his family feared that he might commit suicide if Sheryl broke off their turbulent relationship. His mother, Carol, was at war with Sheryl, who refused to share Paul's Rome villa with his relatives. Other members of the family had lost sleep worrying about Sheryl's influence on Gazza, while she vowed to have nothing more to do with them. She was also furious with jealousy when she discovered he was carrying a torch for TV beauty Donna Derby, then 'Donna the Dart' on Bob Monkhouse's show *Bob's Full House*.

Jane explained that she had left Gazza four months

earlier when he ordered his lawyer Mel Stein to sack her. Jane said Stein told him that the rift had been caused by Sheryl Kyle.

In the tell-all biography, Jane continued: 'Despite his problems, Gazza was an instant hit with Italian women on his first visit to Rome, while Sheryl was back in England. They flocked to his side as the carefree star enjoyed the night life while recovering from a knee injury. His two minders were left exhausted on two hours sleep a night as Paul went boozing and clubbing into the early hours. One night, two local women were provided for his entertainment—one a striking blonde dressed in skin-tight black stretch trousers with wide lacing up the sides. His father, John, had become concerned about his son's night-time habits—and decided it would be wise to remind him about safe sex.'

So, he and Jane dashed to a local chemist to buy a packet of condoms for Gazza's next night out. They delivered them to him when he was lunching at the Rome Hilton. He immediately blew one up and put it over his head. Gazza was notorious for his antics. On one occasion he wrapped himself in loo roll pretending to be an Egyptian mummy. On another he told Sergio Cragnotti: 'Your daughter—bit tits!'

With 'Five Bellies' he would tour Rome's notorious red-light district around the Flaminio Stadium, where spectacular South American transvestites ply their trade. Then there were the girls who hung around outside the gates of the Campo Tommaso Maestrelli, the training ground of the Società Sportivo Lazio. Sheryl would drive out there in her Lancia Y10 and park under the trees across the road to observe her Paul's departure.

Jane Nottage provided deeper insights into Gazza's psychology. It seems that, after witnessing a friend being killed by a car when he was twelve, Gascoigne slept with the lights on.

'It is a problem Sheryl Kyle has tried to conquer,' Jane said. 'She is trying to wean him off his fear of the dark, stop his self-induced vomiting and she comforts him when he has nightmares.'

Nottage said that Gazza had once depended on his former manager at Newcastle United, Glenn Roeder, but he had left to manage Watford when he could no longer put up with Gazza's infantile behaviour. When he left, Sheryl stepped in.

Gazza responded to Jane's book with a smear campaign, claiming that she fancied him and was jealous of his relationship with Sheryl.

'Of all the emotions I feel for Gazza, lust is not one of them,' said Jane. 'He has seriously misunderstood my intentions when I sent him good luck cards or chocolates when he scored a goal. I treated him like the younger brother I never had.'

Despite the press coverage Jane's book had given her, Sheryl's stunning good looks could always be depended on to push her off the front page of the tabloids. When Gascoigne signed a £3-million boot deal with the Italian company Lotto, Sheryl stole the show. Her spectacular entrance turned all the heads in the Piccadilly showrooms and photographers busily snapping Gazza hastily switched their focus to her.

Sheryl then gave him a makeover, getting him to add nearly two hundred eighteen-inch hair extensions to his curly thatch at an exclusive London salon. She helped choose the brown, honey blonde and strawberry blonde locks that cost him £300 to have attached. She said she thought it made him look much sexier.

7

Smashing Wagstory

It clearly did the trick. On 29 August 1993, the *People* announced that Gazza planned to marry 'his sexy free-spending girlfriend Sheryl Kyle—against the advice of his furious family'. Some of them were even considering boycotting the wedding.

'But when it comes to the crunch they will probably back down,' a friend said. 'After all, blood is blood even if they don't see eye to eye with Sheryl. But the fact that she didn't go to his sister's wedding last year has not been forgotten. Typically, Sheryl has already said she fancies a Caribbean cruise for the honeymoon.'

However, relations between Sheryl and Gazza's family remained cool. Earlier that month Gazza's parents John and Carol had invited friends to share an all-expenses-paid holiday with them at their son's £2-million villa on the outskirts of Rome. But when the Geordie party went out for a meal, Sheryl sat on her own table away from the family and their friends.

One said: 'We took over some cases of Newcastle

Brown Ale but she didn't seem keen on joining in."

The newspaper said that big-hearted Paul was so smitten with Sheryl that he didn't bat an eyelid over her spending and was determined to make the match last forever.

'I have a wonderful personal life with Sheryl,' he said. 'We are very happy and madly in love.'

But one of his family's closest friends said: 'His parents, who live modestly, can't understand the amount of money she spends.' Yet his marriage plans were undimmed. Back in England on his way to a World Cup game against Poland, Gazza visited a jeweller in Newcastle. When an assistant asked if he wanted to look at engagement rings costing up to £12,000, Gazza told her: 'I've already chosen one, thank you.'

Instead he splashed out £1,090 on an eternity ring for his sister Anna-Maria, who had just given birth to a boy. Shop assistant Dawn Ward said: 'He came in with Sheryl, his dad, sister Lyndsay and her boyfriend Darren. Sheryl and Paul had their arms around each other and were obviously in love.'

So much so that he valued their privacy. Gascoigne hit a paparazzo who tried to photograph them when they were visiting a lingerie boutique near the Spanish Steps in Rome three months later. Gazza said: 'I thought my private life could have been easier here.'

They flew home when his father John walked out

on his mother Carol. In a surprise move, Sheryl stepped in as a mediator.

It wasn't until 12 March 1994, that news of Sheryl and Gazza's nuptials finally came through. The *Daily Mirror* reported that he wept tears of joy when Sheryl accepted his proposal during a candle-lit dinner at a posh London restaurant. It was described as a 'very emotional, very happy and very moving occasion'. Gazza had laid on a stretch limousine decked out with a hundred red roses to take Sheryl to Le Gavroche, a Michelin-star restaurant in Mayfair, from their home in Hertfordshire. They arrived at 11pm and left three and a half hours later after Gazza recited a love poem he had written and memorised. Their chauffeur carried a cake decorated with the words 'Will you marry me?' which was specially made by the restaurant.

'The cake was in the shape of a heart and the waiter placed it on our table,' said Sheryl. 'Then I saw the words 'Will you marry me?' which had been piped on. It came completely out of the blue. I had no idea he was going to propose like this, but I said 'Yes' straight-away and it was very romantic. All I will say is that we are very excited and very happy.'

She was wearing a chic check suit and he was smartly kitted out in a light blue jacket and slacks for the occasion.

'It was the most romantic thing in the world,' she said. 'The tears were just rolling down my face.'

A friend said: 'There were a lot of people in the restaurant and both Paul and his girlfriend were crying, there was a lot of happiness. I think it has been in the offing for a long time. Paul has had a lot of work commitments but has been trying to arrange to make his relationship with Sheryl a permanent one by marrying her.

'Despite his image he really is a shy man. Although they have been together for a long time, I think he had to pluck up the courage to ask her.'

It cost him. He was faced a fine from Lazio for staying an extra day in England. On the other hand, for once Gazza behaved with decorum. Only two weeks earlier Sheryl had sat by in the restaurant in Rome when Gazza order an extra plate of pasta which he tipped over the head of a mate who had fallen asleep with his head on the table.

After their engagement Sheryl had to nurse Gazza when he broke his leg during training. This made him so grumpy that he flung a glass of brandy across the cabin on a flight to London until she calmed him down. After a forty-five-minute operation, they flew on Concorde to New York. Just weeks later, when they returned to Rome, they broke up after a furious row where she called him 'fat and ugly'. The wedding plans were put on hold. But soon Gazza was bombarding Sheryl with tearful phone calls begging for her to take him back.

'When Paul told us he had broken up with her we cracked open a bottle of champagne,' said a relative. 'But as we were knocking it back and celebrating Paul was pouring his heart out to Sheryl. The first afternoon he came home he called her twice. We couldn't believe it. We thought it was all over.'

Gazza had got very depressed over the breakup.

'He can't bear the thought of not seeing Sheryl again,' he said. 'And he misses her kids like mad. We all really liked the kids. It's not their fault their mum is so horrible.'

Gazza's mum and dad, Carol and John, tried to persuade him that he was better off without her.

'The family don't like her, never have and never will. She hates us and his Geordie pals,' said the relative. John and Five-Bellies flew out to see him. 'This started more problems with Sheryl. Paul was out drinking with them and once again she got fed up. In the end, John was forced to go back home.'

John then endorsed Jane Nottage's controversial biography.

'John was perfectly happy. As long as it was anti-Sheryl, he and the rest of the family were only too pleased,' said Jane. 'They felt Sheryl had Paul under a spell. And whatever they did or said didn't really get through to him.'

Jane said Sheryl once boasted to her that Gazza was hooked because their sex life was so good. 'He'll never leave me,' she said.

Daily Mirror agony aunt Marjorie Proops told the soccer star to eat and drink less and seek the help of a therapist.

'And the last thing you must do is jump under the duvet into another sexual relationship just to stick two fingers up to Sheryl and prove you are Mr Macho Man,' she said. 'Don't, please don't, jump into a relationship on the rebound.'

Instead he took a fishing trip in Scotland. The following month, he gave a lengthy and emotional interview to the *News of the World* where he admitted beating up his former fiancée.

'I hit her because she wasn't paying me any attention, so I thought she didn't love me,' he said. He told the paper he slapped her and pulled her hair, leaving her with heavy bruises. Telling of his jealous rages, he said: 'I've been a violent bastard and a coward and I want the world to know it.'

The paper says Gascoigne called Rebekah Wade, then its features editor, saying he wanted to 'bare his soul' about the breakup. Wendy Clarke, a friend, said that the confession was part of a desperate bid to win Sheryl back.

He broke down sobbing as he told how he once smashed Sheryl's head against a wall. Once, when he had been drinking, Sheryl gave him a peck on the cheek and he immediately thought she'd been with someone else.

'I'd end up arguing with her and then I'd fight her, slap her,' he said. 'When I used to get aggressive with her, like, I'd grab her by the back of her head, pull her hair back and bang her head. She'd cry out: 'Stop it! Please stop it! I can't take any more'. My obsession and jealousy with Sheryl would ruin everything.

He confessed to holding her by the hair as he slapped her face and in one screaming row, he hurled a chair through a window.

'When I saw the bruises the next day I couldn't believe that I had done that to her,' he said. 'I was always devastated. I'd beg and plead and promise: 'Never again.' Then it would happen again. When I got mad, she just froze. She was terrified.'

He told Wendy he needed to admit 'what a horrible bastard' he was to Sheryl.

'By admitting the violence it's the only way I'll get better,' he said. 'My mates are going to slaughter me when they read this. I know what they'll say: "All the time we thought he was good, but he was a bastard." I was so horrible, but I needed to say it… to admit what a horrible bastard I was to her. By admitting the violence, it's the only way I'll get better… I'm so sorry… such a bastard…'

A close family relative said: 'This will be the ruin of Paul. Nobody likes a woman-beater. His fans will turn against him.'

He explained that he would explode at her on holiday because he could not relax with the pressure he was under. 'I just sat back and let Sheryl take all the blame,' he said.

Nevertheless, Gazza continued to insist that Sheryl was his soul mate. He sought psychiatric help and threatened to quit football to open a bar in Australia.

A former neighbour and close friend of the couple told the *People*: 'Paul is still deeply in love with Sheryl and would do anything to have her back. He hopes she can find it in her heart to forgive him.'

He was contrite.

'I've let Sheryl and the kids down,' he said. 'I've let her family down, my family down and even let my club Lazio down. I never want to put Sheryl or anyone through that again. It's just a shame it took me three years to realise it. I'm worried that if Sheryl and I are with each other again, people will wonder why she wants to see me after all this.

'Sheryl was the perfect woman for me when I met her. I want three kids as soon as possible. I don't know whether we'll get back together, but I'd like us to be close friends and work towards a better relationship in the future.'

And he sought to make it up to her.

'The last time Sheryl took me back on condition I agreed to get psychiatric help from a sports psychologist,' he said. 'If I don't sort it out, I'm going to be a very, very lonely person.'

It appeared to be working.

'It was great at first,' he said. 'He was telling me situations and how to deal with it when you get wound up.'

Gazza also explained that he panicked whenever Sheryl lapsed into a self-contained silence lasting more than a few seconds. She was supposed to exist in a constant state of red alert for Gazza's needs. He had come to realise that her attention sometimes lapsed because she was tired.

He was said to have wept after the split at his birthday party while among family and close friends. But soon there were rumours of a reunion when he spent a day together at the seaside with Sheryl and the kids. Her children reportedly pestered their mother to let them keep seeing him.

Sobbing, Gazza told the *News of the World*: 'I had someone to hug and cry on when my football wasn't good, but I abused that… Instead of being a man and having a go at the people who I should have had a go at, I took it out on Sheryl.'

Gazza agreed to a self-imposed injunction barring him from molesting her. His lawyers had drawn up a twenty-five-page 'kiss-off' deal after a previous bust-up. Under it, she would keep the house in Stanstead Abbotts and £30,000 in cash. In return, Sheryl would be gagged for ten years from talking about her turbulent relationship with Gazza in case it damaged him commercially. The agreement went unsigned as the couple had meanwhile got back together again.

'Sheryl loved me so much that she'd take me back. But then something would happen in my mind and it would go off again,' he said. 'Once at a barbecue I saw her talking to neighbours. I lost my temper and started kicking the backs of her legs hard and grabbing her arms. I even got jealous of Sheryl's son Mason sleeping on his mother's knee.'

He was in danger of losing everything he values.

'Our relationship was perfect at first. I had something and I didn't know how to cope with it. It was the first time someone like that was really in love with me. Sheryl is so beautiful. When she agreed to marry me, I was so pleased. But I let her down again,' he said. 'I needed to admit what a horrible bastard I was to her. I'd be nice to everyone else and horrible to Sheryl. I should have protected her as a man should. The worst experience I've ever had is seeing my own fiancée frightened of me…. I want to be a top-class footballer again and a MAN.'

There were fears that Gazza might kill Sheryl during one of these spates and her ex-husband Colin sought to get his kids away from Gazza away as part of a long and bitter custody battle. He complained that even his birthday cards to his children have been returned unopened.

Meanwhile Gazza sought to make amends.

'I've told so many lies to so many people about what went on between me and Sheryl that if we're ever to have a chance of getting back together I've got to tell the truth,' he said.

Other footballers rallied to his support.

'You can't condone what's he done, but I feel a lot of sympathy for Gazza and, of course, for Sheryl,' said Liverpool goalkeeper David James. 'He's always under a lot of pressure and it sounds like she's been through some bad times with him. It's taken a lot of guts to admit it. He's a man to do that because he could easily have said nothing.

Spurs midfielder Mickey Hazard agreed: 'First and foremost, you just can't condone what he's done. Hitting a woman isn't right, not at all. But it takes a lot of guts for him to come out and say what he's said. Hopefully now he can start to put that right and get back together again with Sheryl, because he's a very nice guy.'

Even Argentinian bad boy Diego Maradona rode to the rescue.

'Don't blow it—the soccer world needs you,' he said. 'The world needs players like Paul Gascoigne. Please don't spoil your chances of greatness.'

Gazza's confession sent reporters dashing to Sheryl's front lawn. She called him at his home just two miles away. He came and told them to clear off. He said he was desperate for a reconciliation and he sought to appease her by 'putting the record straight'.

'It was something I had to do to protect Sheryl. I know she got a lot of flak from everybody,' he said. 'We are still friends. I don't regret what I said, but I do regret what I did.'

Could they get back together?

'It's what me and Sheryl have got to discuss,' he replied.

Meanwhile women's groups were demanding he be prosecuted for want amount to a two-year reign of terror. He did not savour their intervention in what he considered to be a personal matter.

'I have said what I have to say,' he said. 'Now I would like everybody to leave us alone and respect our privacy.'

But their troubles continued to be a matter of public record. Sheryl told the *Daily Mirror*: 'I can't stop loving him. I'm devastated about the fuss his confession has caused but deep down I still love him.'

A close friend told the newspaper: 'It is because Sheryl loves Paul so much that she stayed with him to try to make it work. That is why it was so hurtful when people suggested she was only with him for his money. If only they had known the truth.'

She has not ruled out a rapprochement.

'I know she does not see it as an impossibility,' the friend said.

The *Mirror* then polled its readers whether Sheryl should give him another chance. Nine out of ten voted no.

Sheryl did not take their advice. She took him back on a week's trial, though they would sleep in separate beds in his villa and she would take a girlfriend along as a chaperone to make sure Gazza obeyed the rules.

'The tiniest step out of line and she'll be on the first plane home,' said her friend. 'Sheryl still loves Paul and is impressed by how he laid it on the line and publicly admitted he attacked her. But she wants to be sure he is a changed man before she commits herself to him again.'

If it worked out, the couple would then take a three-week holiday with the kids in the South of France.

It appeared that he had won her back with a series of candlelit dinners. They were spotted cuddling together on the terrace of the Fish and Eels restaurant near his £200,000 home at Hoddesdon, Hertfordshire.

'His love for her shone through,' a friend said.

His parents were not so happy though.

'It's no secret they don't like Sheryl. They were rejoicing about the split,' said a family friend. They would have been heartened when Sheryl told the *Daily Mirror* that she had no plans for a reconciliation.

'The stuff I've read in the papers is wrong,' she said as she returned to their Hertfordshire home. 'How can they say this when Paul is not here? He has been in Switzerland for the past three weeks and I have not even seen him.'

However, the following day, she was seen at Heathrow, boarding a plane for Italy. Wearing a blue denim jacket and a short denim skirt, she tried to hide behind airline staff. Ignoring all questions, she remained totally silent. Nevertheless, she took her dark glasses off when photographers moved in.

The *Daily Mirror* said the reunion came with a hefty price tag. British Airways tickets for herself and the children cost over £1,000, while the chauffeur-driven limo set her back another £180. But it seemed to have worked. Two weeks later she was seen at Heathrow again, this time wearing a discreet off-white jacket and keeping her head down. But she could hardly escape the attention of the press as she was accompanied by Gazza in a purple suit as they made for the Nice-bound plane.

When they returned to England, Gazza booked a fleet of nine limos to take her, her kids and a party of friends home in an effort to impress. Even for Sheryl this seemed a little excessive. She cancelled them and paid a £120 for a minibus instead.

The limo hire boss said: 'This is a trial period for Paul and Sheryl. They are trying to patch things up. But Sheryl doesn't like glitz and glamour. She hates all the attention she and Paul get. For her, this was completely over the top.'

A few hours later, Gazza flew in from Rome. He then hired a Cadillac to take them for a candlelit meal in London. They spent that night in the Dorchester.

'Paul would do anything to get her back,' a friend said.

There was a way to go though. Speaking on Channel 4's *Gazza's Italian Diaries*, he said: 'We haven't got back together yet. We haven't really spoken about it, and I'm just happy the way things are. I had some problems and I was taking them out on the person I loved. I don't want Sheryl to get stick, it's not fair for a woman to take that. It was very hard on her. I felt sorry for her in the end.'

Inevitably he put a foot wrong. He forgot to renew the insurance on the £28,000 BMW 325 convertible he bought her for Christmas. She was fined £400 and got an endorsement on her driving licence.

Gazza then went on his friend Danny Baker's late-night Saturday chat show and told listeners that he was not easy to live with and that he had not found a new romance since his split with Sheryl.

'I don't fall in love easily, sometimes I don't know what love is,' he said. 'But I don't want to be alone all my life.'

While he was in London on Danny Baker's show, his Roma villa was broken into and the burglars got away with more than £22,000 worth of goods, including a £800 shocking-pink checked Versace jacket he had bought on a shopping trip with Sheryl among other designer clothes.

Sheryl herself was not keeping a low profile, turning up at the British Hairdressing Awards sporting her own hair-raising creation piled into a knotted bun at the back of her head and a low-cut gown.

'Clearly not to be outdone by the glitterati surrounding her at London's Grosvenor House Hotel, she showed off more crystals round her neck than those decorating the chandeliers,' said the *Daily Mirror*. 'But if Sheryl, 29, was thrilled to be away from her wayward former lover, she didn't show it. The hard stare on her heavily made-up face was more of a look that could kill.'

The paper hazarded a guess that Gazza was not with her because the hairdressers' convention did not serve lager.

With the rift seemingly complete, Gazza put the house he had shared with her and the kids at Dobbs Weir on the market for £189,000. She said: 'He can do what he likes. I don't have anything to do with him.'

But in March 1995, they were again seen together in a smart West End restaurant. Back at Sheryl's £200,000 home in Stansted Abbots afterwards, he denied suggestions there had been a rapprochement.

'Where did you get that information?' he said. 'That's a load of balls. Now f*** off.'

Soon after, they were seen emerging from top London restaurant, Langan's Brasserie, together. When the *Daily Mirror* sought him about for an interview after he forked out £7,500 for thumping a railway signalman in a late-brawl, they found him at Sheryl's house again. He answered the door in a white dressing gown and denied everything. Then he snapped: 'Are you going to f***off or am I going to throw a f***ing brick through your window?' He picked up a stone and snarled: 'If I see you around at the house again, you'll get a brick thrown at you.'

The following month, Sheryl was seen in the stands at Lazio. She was unhappy to see that he had shaved his hair off. Lazio were unhappy too and dropped him because the pressure over his private life was affecting his performance. Gazza himself found the media attention intrusive.

'I would go to nice restaurants with Shez and when I walked in, I knew straight away that the waiters were already ringing the newspapers,' he said. 'Wherever we went, even with the kids Mason and Bianca, the cameramen were there. At the coast, every time we went to the beach or restaurants. It just made you feel like going straight home.

'We once went to EuroDisney and Mason got tired. He was only three and I explained who the cameramen were. Otherwise he was going to start worrying. I told him I'd put him in his pushchair and wheel him around.

But he said: 'No I don't want to be in the papers in a pushchair.' God, three years of age and he's talking like that! I felt like crying for him.'

Gazza's planned to move to Rangers in 1995 in an effort to rekindle his relations with Sheryl who was keen to move to Scotland with the kids. They flew to Sardinia to discuss the £4.5-million transfer deal. But his new £20,000-a-week job was overshadowed by Sheryl with a story that the *Sun* ran under the headline 'Gazza's Shazza hazza big new brazza'. He had paid out £3,000 to have Sheryl's breasts enlarged to 36D.

Even so, Sheryl was lost in the crowd when Gazza turned up for a press reception at Ibrox. He then promised fans to give the booze the boot, after downing a champagne cocktail for breakfast.

'I've not had a beer for months,' he said. Clearly this did not mean that he had foresworn champagne and wine. Asked if he wanted tea or coffee the Geordie lad replied: 'I'll have a Kir Royale.'

The following month it was announced that Sheryl was two months pregnant. 'Gazza to be a Dadda' screamed the headline of the *Sun*. His mother Carol described the news as 'wonderful'.

'Both Paul and Sheryl are over the moon and can't wait for the baby to be born,' she said. 'He's great with kids—Sheryl's two adore him—and he'll be a great dad.'

His father John was said to be 'cool' about the

news. A pal on Tyneside said: 'John has never talked much about Sheryl, though we got the impression he didn't approve of her. Let's hope a baby will change things—that it will mend any differences and also help Paul to settle down.'

A friend of the couple said: 'It's the classic divide between a middle-class Southern girl and working-class Northerners. There has been some ill feeling and it has caused Paul a lot of grief. There's no doubt he's hoping a baby will bring them all together.'

Sheryl said: 'I am very pleased. I have known about the baby for a month and a half. I have told my parents and they are pleased as well. I don't mind what sex the baby is as long as it is healthy. My other two children are looking forward to having a brother or sister.'

Asked about Gazza's new peroxide coiffeur, she said: 'We are in competition. In fact, his is a nicer blond than mine.'

While she insisted that the baby was planned, Gazza was far from pleased. Later in his autobiography, he said he cried: 'Oh shit. That's the last f**king thing I need. I was a total bastard.'

Later he recanted.

'I know it was horrible. It's not the way to behave when your girlfriend's pregnant,' he said. 'I should have given her a hug. I even suggested an abortion, but she refused to consider it.'

He then asked Sheryl to marry him again and

exploded when she turned him down. Understandably she was upset by his behaviour.

'I was devastated that he didn't seem interested in the baby we'd longed for,' she said. 'I feel hurt and let down. I have been finding it hard to cope with what's being said at the moment.'

But Sheryl said he would give Gazza one final chance.

'I want to try—we're agreed about that,' she said.

Gazza was more upbeat.

'We're starting afresh, we're going to enjoy this together,' he said. 'We speak every day and haven't split up.'

'We'll sort it out—we always do. We're very much in love,' she said. 'We are going to try to make a go of it. Now there's a baby involved we have to think about that.'

She told the *People* that she had broken the news while the couple were travelling by limousine to the airport for a holiday in America. She said Paul was busy scribbling out a list of personal essentials needed for his move from Lazio to Rangers, when she blurted out: 'You'd better add a cot to that list!'

Gazza simply asked: 'What? You're pregnant then?' He wrote 'cot' on the list and carried on scribbling.

'I was astonished by his reaction because we'd been so desperate to have a baby,' she said.

Gascoigne told the newspaper: 'I'm furious how I

reacted. I was shocked, like all blokes, that I was going to be a daddy. When I realised it was for real, I was stunned.'

Asked why he had reacted so badly to the news, she said: 'I don't want to discuss that.'

Sheryl then revealed how Paul's friends called him Jaffa when she hadn't got pregnant earlier—because they thought he was seedless.

While Gazza was settling in Scotland, he was said to be singing: 'When I've had a couple of drinks on a Saturday night Glasgow belongs to me.' He had also signed a £200,000 deal with a daily tabloid. Meanwhile Sheryl stayed at home in Stanstead Abbotts.

'I don't know when we will be seeing each other,' she said.

Asked for 'Glazza' Gazza's thoughts on the pregnancy, she said: 'I can't really speak for Paul about how he feels.'

There were concerns that her recent boob job may prevent her breast-feeding, though experts took told the tabloids saying that there should be no problem.

A different tale was told by Gazza's old mate Glenn Roeder, then manager of Watford.

'Paul rang me more than a week before the news was announced that he and Sheryl are having their first baby in February,' he told the *Sunday Mirror*. 'I have never heard Paul so excited about anything. I was thrilled to hear his news and he was absolutely ecstatic.

He will make the ideal parent. He already idolises Sheryl's two youngsters Bianca and Mason. And he will absolutely adore his own child—whether it's a girl or a boy.'

Roeder added: 'There's no way I can see him spoiling the baby with over-expensive gifts.'

The following day, the *Daily Mirror* reported: 'Gazza goes on £14,000 shopping spree.' He told a stunned shop assistant: 'Don't worry, it's only a week's wages for me.'

Glasgow's trendy store Cruise, which had a sponsorship deal with Rangers, closed the store to prevent him being mobbed while he made his pick of clothes by designers such as Armani, Moschino, Paul Smith and Hugo Boss.

Still determined to patch things up with Sheryl, he turned up in twenty-seven-foot stretch limo to take her on a romantic night out. Behind the smoked glass windows, there were £20,000 worth of extras, including a TV video bar and music system. A trip back to Glasgow in it would have cost £800.

He emerged from the $120,000 Cadillac wearing a baggy lilac Versace suit costing £1,000 topped off with a £300 cream waistcoat, a white shirt at £150 and a £80 printed silk tie.

'Soccer star Paul Gascoigne spent a fortune trying to look like Prince Charming as he set out to woo back girlfriend Sheryl Kyle—but he ended up looking more like the Sugar Plum Fairy,' said *Daily Mirror* fashion director Ollie Picton-Jones. 'Pastels shades are the very latest thing for this summer, but with his newly peroxide-dyed hair, Gazza looks far too pale to carry off this colour. The off-the-peg suit definitely needs some tailoring to fit the Clown Prince of Football. He looks more like Coco the Clown in this suit. The cuffs are far too long and the trouser hemlines are flapping around his ankles.'

Columnist Roland White joked that the trousers so baggy that he could have kept a family of ferrets down them with Sheryl none the wiser.

Apparently, Sheryl did not share this opinion and their fresh start began with Gazza slashing £34,000 off the price of his four-bedroom Hertfordshire bachelor pad—complete with whirlpool and en-suite bathrooms—to move in to her £135,000 love nest. His house in Dodds Weir had been on the market at £189,000, but he accepted £154,995 for a quick sale.

A close friend said: 'Paul decided there was no point having two homes just a couple of miles apart."

While the doings of WAGs are usually the fodder of tabloids, the *Sunday Times* could not resist getting in on the latest episode of the Gazza-Shezza soap.

'We are not witnessing a couple on the verge of a split, but the opening act of a story that is going to run and run,' the broadsheet said. 'And with the pair already establishing themselves as the new royal couple for

Glasgow's tabloids, the season ahead looks set for the unfolding of a human drama of truly soap-opera proportions.'

The *Sunday Times* were particularly impressed with Sheryl, saying: 'A former model, Kyle, with legs that go all the way up to the lighting gantry and the blondest Baywatch hair, is a suitable star. And like all put-upon heroines, she's not one to suffer in silence.'

Citing her blow-by-blow account of her feelings given to a trusted interviewer at the *News of the World*, the *Sunday Times* said: 'Clearly, Kyle isn't about to end the storyline when it's just getting going. And there's no shortage of material to feed it. Kyle can draw on a host of personal experiences that would out-soap any *Brookside* or *EastEnders*. Gascoigne's previous mea culpas to allegations that he beat her would sit easily in 'Men Who Abuse Their Partners and The Women Who Still Love Them' storyline. 'Woman Who Is More Intelligent Than Her Lover' would be another plot Kyle could do on autopilot. 'Uptown Girl Chooses Working-Class Boy' would be an equal cinch (some of Gazza's Geordie family are said to think that Kyle, from the southern middle-classes, is a snob).'

She had developed an independent and dominant personality, changing from being 'a prim lady who dismissed women with streaked hair as 'slagbags' into becoming a 'super-glamorous dolly bird'. She had expensive tastes and went on shopping trips for jewellery while she was in Italy.

'One tactic the footballer tried to patch up their pregnancy row was to offer shopping sprees in Cartier and other exclusive shops on Rodeo Drive, Los Angeles,' the newspaper said. 'The ploy failed, but Kyle, who turned down a fleet of nine limousines ordered for her personal use during another rift, speaks of it with a kind of awe.'

It took the *People* to put things back into proportion. It asked Gazza if he was as good in bed as he was on the football pitch. 'Er… you'll have to ask Sheryl about that,' he replied.

But the *Sunday Times* could not let it go. In the run-up to the 1995 season, it did a quick rundown on WAG profiles.

'Where they go: it used to be Tramp and Stringfellows, dancing and drinking until the early hours. Now it is more likely to be lunch at Daphne's in Chelsea or dinner in Harvey Nichols,' the paper said.

Because their other halves were playing abroad, they had turned to French and Italian designers—though while others favoured the understated elegance of Armani, Sheryl had stuck with the more adventurous Versace creations. They had given up burgers and liquid lunches for new wave Italian. Fellow WAG Rachel Platt and her husband David had even bought their own little Italian restaurant Amici Mai in Wolverhampton.

Shag-piles in Essex were out. Shelley Webb had opted for a two-hundred-year-old cottage when she moved to Manchester, while the Linekers moved from an exclusive London townhouse to a £1-million country pile in Buckinghamshire. But then Shelley Webb, Michelle Lineker and Rachel Platt were in the first team, while Sheryl had briefly been relegated to the subs bench.

Things got worse for Sheryl when it emerged that Gazza had partied heavily during their breakup the previous year. He had been in the Raj Gate Indian restaurant in Hoddesdon with his mates Cyril Martin and Terry Bailey, the estranged husband of former glamour model and TV beauty Linda Lusardi.

After a bottle of champagne, they started chatting up twenty-six-year-old blonde Tricia Dolan. She said, 'He asked me for a kiss. I gave in'. Meanwhile Bailey and Martin also cuddled her.

Tricia claimed that Gazza had tricked her while she was drunk and insisted that she only cuddle d Gazza and Bailey.

After the party at the Raj Gate restaurant, Gazza said he felt sick and broke down in tears, but his mate Cyril told him that he couldn't live like a monk. He made a tearful confession of his night out to Sheryl when they patched up their romance.

'I just want to start a new life with her. I wish this had never happened,' he said.

A friend said: 'Sheryl met Trish in a local gym and listened in amazement as Trish told her everything. At first she was furious but in the end she felt sorry for her and said she could help her make some money—by selling her story to the papers.'

Meanwhile WAGs Sheryl and Lusardi had their own problems. After Lusardi and Bailey had split up, she had fallen out with Sheryl.

'Terry's a good-looking boy and it didn't help when Sheryl made it very plain that she fancied him,' a friend said. 'Linda didn't like that way Sheryl kept looking at him and their friendship broke up.'

Dancer Nancy Sorrell, one of Gazza's exes who had just broken up with Steve Coogan, explained: 'I adore Gazza—he's great fun to be with and knows how to treat a lady. He can't resist blondes.'

However, she said, it was not so much fun when he brought 'Five Bellies' along on dates. It seems that Gazza never scored with Nancy. Back in 1991, they slept together in a hotel room, but as Nancy was just seventeen at the time, Gazza—ever the gentleman—forwent the pleasure as she was too young. This must have come as a relief to Sheryl.

Once again Sheryl accepted Gazza's apology and he sought to ingratiate himself by organising a special pre-birthday treat for her at Langan's Brasserie. He hoped it would make up for the time Sheryl had failed to invite him to a champagne party at her home after the couple had fallen out. Ironically, Tricia had been invited and went to the bash.

The strategy seems to have worked. The following week, while they were celebrating her thirty-first birthday over family Sunday lunch at Danesfield House Hotel in Medmenham, Buckinghamshire, Gazza sank to his knees and asked her to marry him once more. She said yes. They embraced and ordered champagne. He was wearing a suit and tie, she a stunning black dress. They had arrived the previous night in a hired limousine which picked Gazza up from Heathrow Airport after he flew down from the Rangers defeat by Hibs at Ibrox.

The couple retired to the £350-a-night honeymoon suite where Gazza had laid on a £120 bottle of 1985 Dom Perignon champagne. Two dozen red roses—a snip at £48—had been arranged on the bedside table, with a note from Sheryl's kids which read: 'Happy Birthday Mummy, With Love From Bianca and Mason.'

Gazza later told a hotel porter: 'I'm very happy. I'm getting married.'

'It was all so romantic,' said a staff member. 'Gazza was in a great mood. He'd had a few drinks and was in really high spirits. Near the end of the meal, he suddenly went down on his left knee beside her with arms open. I thought he was about to start singing. But he said, 'Will you marry me?' and Sheryl replied, 'Yes.'

'Gazza looked so happy. And there were smiles all

round from everyone else at the table. The whole restaurant was buzzing.'

Another member of staff said: 'He clearly wanted to do everything in high style.'

The only thing missing was the ring. The following day, Gazza celebrated with his teammates, donning Mel Gibson's *Braveheart* costume complete with woad and kilt. Then the management got serious. A top-secret letter entitled 'Gazza's Wedding—How We Can Make Wads of Dosh" circulated among the board which leaked to the *Daily Record*. Rangers boss David Murray was furious.

Speaking at the official opening of the Gazza Chapel of Love in Govan, Murray said: 'Mr Gascoigne's nuptial arrangements are a strictly private matter between himself and the manager, the players, the club, our supporters, our sponsors, our commercial development manager and our merchandising agents.'

Surely Sheryl should have a say.

'This is another example of the press putting two and two together and coming up with at least £5 million, excluding VAT and possible TV rights,' Murray said.

Rangers' plans included an all-ticket wedding in front of 48,000 people, live coverage exclusively on SkySports and a half-time lucky Order of Service draw.

Sportswear manufacturers Adidas said they had been asked to design a replica wedding kit.

'We are making 100,000 small black morning coats with Gazza's name on the back,' said a company spokesman. 'We have also been asked to make 50,000 blue and white garters for the girls with the club motto 'Ready' as a motif.'

The club's caterers have also been asked to quote for 50,000 horseshoe-shaped Blue Nose Burgers.

Manager Walter Smith had other worries. He feared that Gazza had twisted a knee kneeling to propose to Sheryl and would not be fit to play Borussia Dortmund that night.

Gazza was thinking of buying £375,000 mock-Tudor house in Helensburgh off teammate Mark Hateley but wanted Sheryl to see it before making an offer.

'Once I've found a house with Sheryl and settled down it will be perfect up here,' he said. 'I might even buy a kilt for the wedding!'

The broadsheet said that he liked the package—a simple blonde and a ready-made 'instant pot-noodle family' of two children, while she is 'rather slow to catch on'.

'She always looks a little too tart, like past-the-sell-by-date yoghurt. Yet, he's got her wrong. He's got her, just because she's three years older and with kids, pencilled in as this mummy figure for whom he has quite often yearned. Once he got obsessed with a woman called Karen, a neighbour's wife, because she was so homely.'

The paper pointed out that Sheryl was herself once a neighbour's wife as he lived nearby in Hoddesdon. And Gazza 'particularly likes the cachet in winning another man's woman'.

While they were house hunting, they squatted in a £32,000 luxury timeshare lodge on the banks of Loch Lomond. They were looking in upmarket areas to the west of Glasgow where up-market houses fetched up to £1 million. But the whole thing seemed to be off when Sheryl walked out on him at Quaglino's, a fashionable restaurant in London, when a stunning topless model Sarah Heaney came to their table to say hi. When a row broke out, he told Sheryl: 'Don't f**king embarrass me. I don't need you.'

Paparazzo Nicos was outside the restaurant when she made for the limo.

'She didn't say anything but you could see she was really mad,' he said. 'She just stormed over to the car and got in. When the chauffeur saw me taking pictures, he jumped out and said he was going to kill me.'

Gazza emerged looking dazed a few minutes later.

'He was staggering all over the place,' said the photographer. 'He was seriously drunk and could hardly get up the stairs. He was confused and looking around for the girl but she was well gone. When he spotted me, he said: 'If you take a picture of me, I'll thump you.' One of his friends was more or less holding him up and they helped him back into the restaurant.'

When Gazza finally left the restaurant around midnight, he was smuggled out of the back door into a taxi.

'I managed to get a shot of him in the car,' he said. 'His eyes were half shut. He was very, very drunk.'

While Gazza was trying to avoid the press, Sheryl ran straight into the open arms of the *Daily Record*.

'The girl came over to us in the restaurant and said, "Hi Paul, we met two weeks ago", "I said sorry who are you" and she said she was the girlfriend of someone I had met. I said to her that she wasn't the girl I had seen that man with and she said: "Oh, he's got lots of girlfriends".'

'That's when Paul started abusing me, effing and blinding across the table in front of everyone in the restaurant. He expected me to sit and take all this abuse. The problem is that he is so jealous and possessive he would go absolutely mad if it was the other way round. It's no good anyone telling him, he's got to be the one to make the changes.'

She pointed the finger directly at Gazza. 'He still thinks it's everyone else's fault, my fault for walking out, the girl, the person who introduced him to the girl. It's everyone's fault except Paul Gascoigne's.'

Meanwhile, Sarah Heaney said she planned to sue an English newspaper over the story.

'I'm furious,' she said. 'I don't want to talk about it. The matter is in the hands of my solicitor.'

Her fiancé, Aberdeen defender John Inglis, who she lived with in an upmarket flat in Edinburgh, said: 'There is no story. There is no problem.'

She was also a former girlfriend of Rangers chairman David Murray.

The *Daily Record* knew that, whatever had happened in the present, one man had been football's inky devil from the start.

'It's all George Best's fault. Before he brought his Beatle-cut to Old Trafford, players never strayed from the sports pages,' it complained.

The paper went further. Modern WAGs were to blame. Instead of being mumsy, they were so glamorous they drew the eye away from footballers.

'And if you saw a woman on match day, she had a tea-pot in her hands. Now, the stands are full leggy, lusting ladies. They linger in the post-match lounges hoping to catch the eye of their prey. And if that fails, they'll trail them to a pub, or club.'

This even worked for ugly footballers. But if you were good-looking, 'you can go through more birds than Colonel Sanders'.

Being a WAG was hardly a bed of roses. The *People* reported that Sheryl believed Gazza was having an affair with Scottish beauty Sarah, whom he met recently at a friend's home, and had vowed not to take him back. While Gazza had admitted on cheating on her with Tricia, he denied having an affair with Sarah.

'Gazza is still besotted by Sheryl. He'll do anything to get her back again,' a friend reassured the media once again. He showed her by being protective of her.

Clearly, he was trying to attract her attention when an injured Gazza appeared in the stands wearing a pink suit and yellow waistcoat to watch Rangers play Falkirk.

He was also very protective of her, having paid out £800 to photographer who had tried to take pictures of her. Freelancer Jason Mitchell was waiting outside their Hertfordshire home when they returned with the children. Gazza jumped out of the car and grabbed him by the throat. He seized Mitchell's camera and ripped out the film.

'I was perfectly friendly to start with. Then I caught him looking through a window trying to get a picture of Sheryl and the kids,' said Gazza. 'That made me angry. With Sheryl being so pregnant I am obviously very protective of her. I went out and told him to give me his film and leave us alone. He wouldn't and things got a bit heated. I ended up pulling the film out and throwing his camera down. I just lost my rag—but what man wouldn't, with someone upsetting his girlfriend?

Then the police turned up.

'They were sympathetic and told me the best thing I could do was apologise and offer to pay for damage to the camera,' he said. 'Sheryl didn't think I had anything to apologise for, but I told her: 'I don't need this hassle.'

'So, I went outside and asked how much it would cost to have his camera repaired. He told me £600. Then the cheeky beggar said he would only accept the money if he could also take exclusive pictures of my Sheryl and the kids. I said that was definitely not on. I just wrote him a cheque for £800 and told him to get on his bike.'

Gazza did not escape punishment. He was indicted for assaulting a photographer and damaging his camera in the incident outside the lingerie shop in Rome. This resulted in three-month suspended sentence and £750 in damages.

The violence then extended to the football field with Gazza blatantly head-butting Sarah Heaney's fiancé John Inglis during a Rangers game against Aberdeen fifteen minutes after the kick-off. The referee did not see the incident, but it was witnessed by hundreds on the terraces and thousands on the TV. However, Gazza claimed to be the victim.

'Nobody took any notice when I was spat on,' he said. 'Nobody dwelt on the fact I was punched in the ribs. It was so severe that the doctor had to look at it after the game.'

Procurator-Fiscal's Office in Glasgow asked Strathclyde police to investigate.

It was then noted that Sheryl had abandoned her usual glam glad-rags for a shell-suit and trainers. The *Daily Record* said she seemed content to cover her curves with shapeless sports gear. However, she had just popped out to the local newsagents.

Perhaps impressed by her Geordie look, Gazza splashed out £500,000 on a family home near the small town of Kilbarchan thirteen miles from Rangers' ground. The six-bedroom clematis-clad Edwardian mansion, known as the White House, boasted a swimming pool, tennis court and two acres of gardens. It had a master bedroom with en-suite Jacuzzi and giant walk-in wardrobe, an enormous conservatory and hi-tech security system.'

Clearly the couple had made up. A friend said: 'Gazza fell in love with the place the moment he and Sheryl walked in. The house is perfect and has more than enough room for his growing family. Sheryl was very impressed by it. She has already got plans on how she wants it decorated.

'He put an offer in immediately and it has been accepted. There is some paperwork to organise, but he hopes to move in before Sheryl's baby arrives in February. He's ready to settle down now.'

Really? Just days later Gazza was thrown out of a curry house in Gateshead after singing and swearing. He was refused service and the police had to be called.

Nevertheless, the *Daily Mirror* soon reported that Gazza had spent £315,000 on a five-bedroom house and a nearby flat for family and friends to stay in when they visited. He put down a twenty-four-hour holding deposit on the £212,000 showhouse in Kilmacolm, Renfrewshire, plus another £10,000 for the contents so they could move straight in.

'Paul wants Sheryl and her kids to come to Scotland as quickly as possible and has the show home very much in his sights,' a friend said. 'He just wants to drop his suitcases down and settle into family life.'

The lounge was twenty-two feet long and the dining room thirteen-feet. The five bedrooms were off the gallery staircase and the master bedroom had a separate dressing area and a classy en-suite bathroom with shower.

However, with the baby due, things grew chilly between the couple. During January 1996, he had only seen her three times. In an angry row over the phone, Sheryl asked: 'Do you want to be a father to this baby or not?'

She put the delivery of furniture ordered from Harrods on hold.

'Either he pulls himself together or we're through,' she told friends.

Once again, things were patched up when Gazza went through with the purchase of the White House and Sheryl prepared to move in. It had leaded bay windows and original features. The enormous, wood-panelled hallway was carpeted in royal red and dominated by a sweeping mahogany staircase. The sumptuous living room had colour-washed walls and a fireplace. The stately wood-panelled, chandelier-hung dining room has space to seat all Gazza's team-mates. The airy farmhouse-style kitchen was done out in stripped pine. The bathroom boasted a novel steam shower. A large conservatory is just the place where a lad can relax and grow a few delicate plants. And a sophisticated sound system piped music around the house.

Then there was the impressively regal navy and claret master bedroom with an en-suite Jacuzzi big enough for two and a giant walk-in wardrobe and the lace-trimmed nursery was decorated in Rangers' blue and white, and littered with teddy bears. Views overlook open country. There were security gates opening onto a secluded drive.

'The couple's privacy is virtually guaranteed with a state-of-the art security system that means visitors can be viewed on TV sets throughout the house,' the *Daily Record* said. So, their privacy was guaranteed except, of course, when they want to blab their mouths to the *Daily Record*.

The next problem was whether Gazza would be with Sheryl when the baby was born.

'We're planning for Paul to be there for the birth, although I don't know what will happen if the baby arrives on a match day. It had better not!' said Sheryl.

Then there was the matter of toys. Sheryl and the children accompanied on a shopping trip to Hatfield where Gazza began fooling around with a remote-controlled car.

'They looked like a real happy family,' said a fellow shopper. 'Sheryl kept linking arms with him and they all seemed to be having fun. Gazza looked like a big kid, playing with the remote control.'

8
Wag a Momma

Sheryl was beginning her contractions when Gazza flew down from Scotland. But instead of going to the couple's pile in Hertfordshire, Gazza went out on the lash with his mates in London. When they began to flag, he bragged: 'I'm the one who should be having an early night. My missus is about to drop a sprog. But I'm not worried – I'm up for a few more pints.'

They had started at 7pm in the Punch and Judy pub in Covent Garden. 'Move out the way lads, I need a p***,' he told another drinker.

Egged on by his mates he cuddled and pinched shocked girls' bottoms as he leered into his glass. Singing and swearing, he jumped on a pal's back, crying: 'On the p***, on the p***!'

When he spotted a pair of sexy girls in black mini-skirts clip-clopping up the street in high heels he then pretended to be a snake charmer, desperately wiggling his hips. Recoiling in disgust, one said: 'Ugh, it's that fat bloke Gazza—he couldn't charm the pants off a stripper.'

In the Marquess of Anglesey pub near the Royal Opera House, he stripped off his top and said: 'Look, I've got me t**s oot for the lads!'

After he threw up, he resumed his assault and his hands were all over the girls like an octopus. They told him to get lost.

Gazza moved to Casper's Bar—a well-known pick-up joint in Hanover Square—where one of his mates turned on a reporter, screaming: 'Get the f***ing hell out of here! Gazza's trying to enjoy a night out. Now f*** off before I knock your head off!'

Inside Gazza lapped up the attention from starstruck girls. But one objected to his wandering hands. She said: 'His face looked all red and bloated from the booze. With that horrid pink T-shirt he looked just like an overcooked salmon. What does that Sheryl see in him?'

The party then hijacked a taxi, which happened to be occupied by a reporter from the *News of the World*.

'You don't mind if we share your cab, mate?' slurred Gazza. 'Fancy joining us for a drink?'

They sped back to their posh £150-a-night hotel in Grosvenor Square. Gazza shot straight to the bar and ordered a round of beers. He flirted with the pianist and dragged a bewildered forty-year-old brunette to her feet for a dance, before pouring his heart out to her.

'I was shocked to hear that his fiancée is having a

baby. I can't believe he was flirting with me while she was about to give birth,' she said. 'He even asked me out to dinner and although we're like chalk and cheese we got on really well.'

After another five bottles of beer, he stumbled to the gents, where he fell into a cubicle, keeled over and was sick again.

Afterwards he bawled: 'I'm totally p***ed. My wife's expecting a baby. I want it to be a boy but I don't know what the f*** I'm going to call it. Sorry, mate, I've got to get back to my room quickly.'

At around 1.30am, after the bar staff refused to serve him any more drinks, friends put him to bed. In the morning, he awoke with a thumping headache and could stomach nothing more than a glass of water for breakfast.

During the excesses of the night, Gazza had not phoned Sheryl, eventually turning up on her doorstep at 11.15am. There was a row. After fifteen minutes, he fled, driving to Newcastle to see his dad, though he had vowed to be there for the birth.

'I can't cope!' he announced. 'This waiting's left me a bundle of nerves.'

The aggro took such a toll on Sheryl that her contractions virtually stopped and she was rushed in pain to Queen Elizabeth II Hospital in Welwyn Garden City by her GP.

'The doctors think it's all because of the stress,' she

sobbed to a newspaper reporter. 'This time Paul's gone too far. What he's done is unforgivable. He promised me he'd be by my side in these crucial hours. I'm just about to give birth to his first child and all he wants to do is get drunk with the lads. I need him here with me to hold my hand and tell me everything's OK.'

Nevertheless, she was surprisingly forgiving.

'I know Paul's just a big kid himself. But we've had plenty of time to prepare for this. We even know it's a boy and we are going to call him Regan. Paul has just got to grow up and start facing up to his responsibilities.'

A shamefaced Gazza told the *News of the World*: 'I've been bang out of order. I wanted to be there for Sheryl. But I was so nervous I thought I'd get in the way. Friday was to be my last big blowout before the baby was born. But it turned into a raz and I got p***ed out of my head.'

As a result of his antics, Gazza was three-hundred miles away on Tyneside when Sheryl gave birth to his son. It was said, nonetheless, he was 'chuffed to bits'.

'The fact he wasn't with Sheryl at such an important moment is bound to take some forgiving,' confided a friend. 'She had expected him to share the trauma and joy of childbirth with her.'

Sheryl poured out her heart to the *Daily Mirror*. 'I've had enough of him,' she assured the newspaper. 'I haven't spoken to Paul since giving birth. He hasn't even bothered to call or find out how his son is. I don't know where he is, and I don't care. People can make their own minds up about his behaviour. I'm too busy looking after Regan to worry about him anymore.'

By then, he had driven another 140 miles north to rejoin the Rangers squad. After three days, he turned up with a bouquet of flowers so big that it filled the back seat of his chauffeur-driven car, a teddy bear and another toy for 7lb 4oz Regan, along with a carefully wrapped box of Belgian chocolates for long-suffering Sheryl.

'He was unusually quiet, but he's ecstatic about the baby,' said the chauffeur.

A friend speculated: 'They've a lot of talking to do.'

If that was not bad enough, the police interviewed Gazz over an alleged sex attack in 1994. A friend of Gazza's said: 'He knows this woman and admits they had sex in the past when he wasn't with Sheryl. But any suggestion foul play was involved is absolute rubbish.'

He was not arrested and there were no charges, but this was hardly the recipe for domestic harmony. Sheryl took her case to the *News of the World* so that she could vent her disappointment with the new father. She told the newspaper: 'He loves our child, but he doesn't love me. If he really cared for me, he'd have been there at the birth. Instead he ran back to his family and I went into labour praying right up until the last minutes that he'd come bursting through the doors to hold my hand.'

The *News of the World* got to print the first pictures of Regan who she cradled in her arms.

'When your baby is born it should be a wonderful moment,' she said. 'But when the nurse placed Regan in my arms, I just felt devastated. I was happy he was all right, but the one person I really wanted to be there—and hoped would have wanted to be there—was nowhere to be seen. Then I looked at Regan and saw he had Paul's nose and top lip and the pain welled up inside me again.

'I knew no matter what happened between us now, he'd never get this moment back. It was gone forever. I felt sorry for Paul and me, but especially Regan. Then, when everyone had gone and I was on my own, I started to realise he couldn't have really ever loved me.'

There had been warnings. At the first sign that the baby was ready to be born the previous Tuesday, she had phoned him.

'He was in a Glasgow bar playing snooker and he said: "What do you want me to do? I've missed the last flight to London and I've lent my car to Jimmy ['Five Bellies'] so I can't come down unless I borrow one",' she said. 'I felt disappointed, but I said I'd call him if anything happened. He phoned the next morning—Valentine's Day—and I told him not to worry, the contractions hadn't started. He wasn't on his own mobile, although he'd promised to keep it switched on so I could let him know when the baby started coming.

'Then he told me he'd lent that to Jimmy as well. I got upset and he started hurling abuse at me, so I slammed the phone down on him. That's when I started to ask myself, 'Does he really want to be here?' I already had suspicions because he'd been distant since Christmas.

'I'd hardly seen him. The kids and I were supposed to have moved up to Scotland permanently at Christmas, but he made it clear a few days after that he didn't want us there. And he was spending all his free time with his family and mates in Newcastle.'

The reporter interviewed her in her Hertfordshire home where Gazza's enormous bouquet was left unopened.

'I didn't hear from him Thursday, then he phoned on Friday morning and left a message,' she said as she poured out her heart. 'He said he was coming down to London for a p***-up with the lads from his team. He said I could reach him at the Britannia Hotel. Then the message added, '… but I won't be much use because I'll be rat-a**ed'.

'Then he phoned my friend Ami, who told him the birth was imminent. He said he knew that, but that his mates were relying on him for a good time. He said: 'If I miss the birth, I miss the birth, other people have done it. It's not that bad.'

'By the time I got home at 4pm, my contractions

were just starting, but Paul didn't pick up his hotel messages. I was going frantic. He didn't call once and the pains were almost unbearable. The doctor wanted me to go into hospital, but I put it off. I kept hoping Paul would phone or turn up.'

Instead he was sleeping it off.

'He finally called me at 10.30 the next morning-Saturday because a friend tipped him off that I was in labour,' Sheryl went on. 'I hadn't had a wink's sleep through worry, stress and pain, and he came on and said, "I'm on my way".'

'My contractions started again in the afternoon and the doctor had me taken into hospital at 5.30pm on Saturday. It was horrible. The midwives kept coming over and asking where Paul was. I kept asking what the time was, thinking to myself, 'He'll have arrived in Newcastle by now, his dad will have persuaded him to come back down to me.'

'I never gave up hope even when the doctor was telling me to push. I wanted to drag the labour out in case Paul was on his way. I kept thinking how terribly sad it was that he was missing the birth. Then I turned to Ami and said "I hate him."'

Sheryl gave birth at 6.42am on Sunday morning and got a friend to tell Gazza.

'I still kept thinking he'd come back,' she said. 'I was at the hospital until 5.30pm but he didn't even call. It's one thing for me to know I'm a mug for loving him and staying with him all this time, but I hate everyone else thinking it as well', she told the readers of Britain's largest newspaper.

Sunday night and Monday passed without a call or a card from the new father. Then his sister phoned.

'Anna said Paul wanted my mother to take Regan to a hotel so he could be alone with him,' Sheryl said. 'I couldn't believe what I was hearing. It was snowing outside.'

Gazza finally arrived just after 12.30pm on Wednesday. According to Sheryl, he came up to her bedroom, handed her some chocolates and said: 'I don't suppose you'll want these.' Then he walked into Regan's nursery with silk flowers and a teddy bear.

'He walked over to his little Moses basket and whispered, 'He's lovely', then I shut the door and left them alone,' said Sheryl. 'I sat on my bed and I heard Paul crying quietly. Then he carried Regan out to me and said, "He's lovely, isn't he?"'

Gazza then talked about Sheryl and the kids going back up to Scotland to live with him as a family, but she refused to answer.

'He got annoyed with me and said if I wouldn't go with him, he wouldn't come here to see Regan again,' she said. 'Instead, he'd wait until Regan was old enough to go out of the house without me. He wanted my mother to bring Regan to him so he could take him out. He thinks that's going to be in about two weeks. He's got no idea about caring for a newborn baby.'

That evening Gazza escaped over the back fence so that he would not be seen.

'I still love him,' she said. 'I always will, but I've got to start thinking about my children. Every time something like this happens, I lose a little bit more respect for myself. I didn't take this decision to have a baby lightly. Paul went on at me for two years solidly about having his child and when things were going well between us, I thought it was the right time. All I wanted was his time and his support. But I got neither.'

'Paul's mum and Anna were coming down next week to see Regan, but he's stopped them. And he told me if I send them any photos, he'll just rip them up. I don't know if I can ever forgive him this time. If becoming a father can't make him grow up, what can? I'd love him to read this and know how much he's really hurt me. But once again I'm probably just kidding myself.'

She also confided in her hairdresser, saying: 'I want Gazza out of my hair. This time he's gone too far. If he can't be bothered to turn up to see his first child being brought into the world, then that says something about his priorities in life.'

But Gazza was not finished. When he scored a winning penalty against Aberdeen, he said: 'I did it for my baby son. I hope Sheryl will allow me back. I had to do something for her. I'll put the goal down to the baby—it might get me back in the good books.'

When Regan was returned to hospital with a mild infection, Gazza turned up as soon as he could. A close friend of Sheryl's said: 'This is a very worrying time for her. At least Paul is doing the decent thing by being with her now.'

Nevertheless, he got into an altercation with a photographer, calling him 'a f***ing pervert' for taking pictures. Then Gazza jumped over a hedge and threw a brick at him, striking him on the knee. He protectively told *Mirror* reporter Graham Bough: 'If you come within five or ten yards of Sheryl, I'll break your f***ing neck."

Matters were hardly improved when Gazza was pictured cuddling eleven-week-old Ebony Walls in a Gateshead pub. Her mother Jasmine said: 'Paul was friendly and gentle. I thought what a wonderful father he'd make. It's a shame it was somebody else's baby he was cuddling.'

Sheryl then turned down an invitation to his niece's christening in Tyneside. By May the *News of the World* was given an exclusive and printed pictures of him cuddling Regan. Meanwhile Sheryl was seen at a champagne party given by then *News of the World* deputy editor Rebekah Wade and *East Enders* star Ross Kemp. Gazza had his own drunken party on board a Cathay Pacific flight back from England's tour of the Far East. In-flight TV screens were damaged by Gazza's kung-fu kicks.

By then the rift between Sheryl and Gazza was deepening again with threats of legal action. Three weeks earlier he had turned up at her home drunk.

'He made a lot of veiled threats saying he never wanted to see the kid again and would stop paying money for his upbringing,' revealed a friend. 'Sheryl doesn't want it to end up in court, but she will sue him if he leaves her no alternative'.

Sheryl was so annoyed by Gazza's behaviour that she struck back and had left his name off the birth certificate. She was also furious that he was not there to talk to the reporters who had been staking out her house all week, leaving her to face the music over his boozy jet trip and some drunken exploits at his twenty-ninth birthday party in a nightclub in Hong Kong.

'I feel totally let down by him because he has just vanished,' she said. 'If only he'd said, 'Look, I'm the one you want to talk to, leave Sheryl and the children alone.' But he hasn't and it's as if he has no respect for us.'

A radio silence reigned between the young parents. Gazza had not called her since he had been back. Instead, he checked into Henlow Grange, a £250-a-night health farm in Bedfordshire... then popped out for a few pints at the nearby Crown inn to celebrate his brother Carl's birthday.

Gazza's twenty-ninth birthday bash was featured in

Shelley Webb's 'Soccer Wives Guide to Surviving Euro 96' in the *Daily Mirror*, which gave ten golden rules for Sheryl and other WAGs to follow.

1. Avoid newsagents and paperboy. 'There'll be countless chambermaids, chauffeurs and cooks willing to concoct a tale of footy infidelity. Take it all with a sack—not a pinch—of salt.

2. Forget all dreams of glamour. 'Being an England wife is like being married to a travelling salesman.'

3. Cultivate a keen sense of humour, optimism or stoicism—SOS for short. 'An England wife is like a kit bag, an appendage to her footy fella. If she's lucky, she'll be almost as important as his shin pads. She's the one who mops his brow, pats him on the back, holds his hand and wipes away his tears.

4. Pander to his quirks. 'Footballers can be very superstitious creatures. Forgetting to pack his lucky boxer shorts, favourite pair of socks or tie can have dire results.'

5. Handle them very carefully. 'When a player makes the England squad, it's almost as if they become 'works of art'.'

6. Be flexible—football comes first at all times. She told of Steve Stone's fiancée Judith who had to reschedule her long-planned wedding because it clashed with the Euro 96 final.

7. Don't expect the best seat. 'When England took

on West Germany in the World Cup 90 semi-final, I was sat high in the Turin stadium. Twenty-five million people back home got a better view on their TVs than I did.'

8. Soccer wives don't count. She recounted being stopped by an Italian guard who shooed them away with his gun, shouting: 'Go away you English groupies!'

9. Forget fashion and fly the flag. No true WAG takes this advice.

10. Never forget at the end of the day, it's only a game.

Was Sheryl paying attention?

Reporters again staked out her Hertfordshire home after Gazza's poor form in a 1-1 draw with Switzerland in Euro 96. They spotted Gazza taking Sheryl out for lunch. When they couple returned three hours later, newsmen were subject to a torrent of abuse and obscene gestures from the England star. When a TV crew lobbed him a football, he booted it into a nearby river.

9
The Also-Wags

While Sheryl commanded the WAG waves like no one before her, there was the run-up to England's Euro 96 semi-final against Germany. It briefly focused the attention on the WAGs of the other players, though none could compete with the twists and turns of the Sheryl-Paul soap that kept the nation spell-bound.

Goalkeeper David Seaman had left his wife of ten years for Debbie Rodgers the then part-time receptionist at Arsenal football club. When he moved in with her, she said: 'It was fun for him having no ties and doing what he wanted to.' But she revealed that he did not like getting pictures of naked women in the post.

She never missed a home game and preferred a quiet evening in, to the high life. When David failed to make a vital save against Zaragoza, Debbie told him: 'You're not superman, you can't stop every ball.'

Paul Ince's wife Claire was again criticised for wearing the trousers. 'I'm no iron lady,' she said. 'We make decisions as a family.'

Rachel Platt, married three years, followed husband David when he signed for Italy's Juventus. 'I left home, married and moved all at once,' she said.

Jane Adam, wife of Tony, was praised for sticking by her husband when he went to prison for drink-driving in 1991. Then Tony took his turn to show his support when she went into a London clinic to fight her drug addiction.

'Despite all their problems, Tony adores Jane,' said a friend. 'They have a fabulous sex life. Jane tells everyone what a wonderful physique Tony has.'

Alan Shearer's wife Lainya confessed that she was not a keen football fan, but she watched all her husband's matches.

'My dad had never watched a game in his life either. Now the whole family watch—but I'm only interested when Alan's playing.'

Teddy Sheringham's girlfriend Nicola Smith followed his career and would totally let her hair down while watching, 'When Teddy scored during the Holland game, I jumped around so much that my hair, which had been in a ponytail, ended up all over the place.'

German striker Jurgen Klinsmann had married American model Debbie the previous year. He described her as the most important person in his life, and always blew her a kiss after the National Anthem was played and another when the game ended.

However, the England players had been banned

from seeing their wives and girlfriends until their final match was over. Sheryl arrived at Wembley with Regan in a pink Cadillac to watch Gazza play, but was turned away from Burham Beeches Hotel in Buckinghamshire when coach Terry Venables kept the players corralled.

'I'd like to be able to let them out of the hotel to enjoy themselves they've earned that, but I can't,' he said. 'I think they should be allowed to see their wives, girlfriends and families. But they understand. It's just one more week. The real hope is that they will be able to do exactly what they want after the final next Sunday.'

And not all WAGs sought the relationship with the press that Sheryl had. Stuart Pearce's wife Liz refused an offer of £20,000 from a tabloid newspaper to talk about the nerve-racking ordeal of watching her husband take a penalty after missing, in the 1990 World Cup.

'She turned it down without batting an eyelid,' an FA spokesman said. 'Stuart has asked for privacy for all members of his family to be respected and most of the players feel the same way.'

Marriages were in the air. Nicola Smith was in the Algarve, Portugal, with Teddy Sheringham. Judith Stone was in Barbados with husband Steve Stone. Lainya Shearer was at home with hubby Alan and the kids. Other destinations included Bali, South America, Cyprus, the Cayman Islands and Italy.

10
Wag Wedding

The day after their reconciliation lunch in Hertfordshire, it was finally announced that Paul and Sheryl were to wed on the day after the Euro '96 final, in the hope they could have a double celebration. She then took the kids to watch him play against Scotland at Wembley. Afterwards he phoned her from the England team's hotel and popped the question again. Apparently, he was soon doing this a dozen times a day. As with a royalty wedding, the media kept an blow by blow tally of the preparations, costs and guest list, speculating on the many things that might go wrong on the day.

'Sheryl has ordered her dress and is getting very excited about the big day,' a friend said. 'He says he has been an idiot and is now ready to settle down', the friend added hopefully. In a triumph of hope over experience, Sheryl accompanied him to pick out his wedding outfit in Harrods.

'She wanted to be with him so that he didn't buy

anything too over the top,' said the ubiquitous pal.

South Shields were captivated, said the *Sunday Mirror*, comparing their nuptials to those of Charles and Diana, and Prince Rainier and Grace Kelly. The paper celebrated the couple's forthcoming marriage by mocking up a wedding album, showing Gazza in top hat and tails, looking carefully through the bottom of a champagne bottle at Sheryl in a cream taffeta number.

As Sheryl bore more than a passing resemblance to Pamela Anderson, the newspaper suggested a *Baywatch*-style ceremony, while Gazza's life story could have been written by Hans Christian Andersen.

'While a red swimsuit might be perfect for Malibu, it could get a bit draughty in South Shields,' it pointed out.

The paper also unkindly compared Sheryl to Little Bo-Peep who had lost one particular sheep more times than she cared to remember. The problem was with Gazza's hairstyle resembling a 'peroxide hedgehog', the bride risked being upstaged.

There would be precious little privacy for Gazza and Sheryl's £100,000 wedding at the Hanbury Manor Hotel in Hertfordshire where Sheryl had once worked as a receptionist. Although all its ninety-five rooms had been booked by Gazza for £15,000 to prevent gate crashers, *Hello!* magazine paid £150,000 for exclusive pictures to help defray the expense of the nuptials. And there would be celebs. Gazza had invited drinking pals

Danny Baker and Chris Evans, who forewent his £10,000 fee to DJ at the reception. The England squad and their WAGs would be among the eighty guests and Gazza had arranged for Sheryl to arrive in a horse-drawn carriage—a limo being too run of the mill.

Sheryl was left to make the other arrangements. She wore black jeans and a clinging lemon T-shirt to tie up the paperwork in Hertford register office, paying £214 for a special marriage licence. Meanwhile, in a different part of the world, England were knocked out of Euro '96 and Gazza threw soup over ITN reporter Ben Ando and slammed the door in his face when he turned up at their house.

If that wasn't enough, the police banned the horse-drawn carriage for security reasons. Details of the couple's outfits also leaked. Sheryl would wear a £10,000 Isabell Kristensen silk dress in French lace with salmon netting, a pale pink handed-beaded satin strapless bustier and pink meringue-cum-tutu skirt, while Gazza would be kitted out in a £1,000 cream-and-gold embroidered silk suit and cravat. Tailors Favourbrook were making the knee-length frock coat, trousers and waistcoat in only two weeks. The flamboyant London store normally took two months just to run up a jacket.

A pal said: 'He picked it with Sheryl's approval. It's very flashy and great fun.'

But there was trepidation in the press. Marjorie

Proops said she had to 'confess to grave doubts about the future married life of Mr and Mrs Paul Gascoigne'. She said that Gazza could look after himself, but she was not so sure about Sheryl.

'It beats me why she's at last succumbed to the temptation to marry him,' she said. 'She didn't look all that ecstatic when she emerged the other day from the Register Office…'

In the *Sun*, ex-Page 3 girl Linda Lusardi told Sheryl: 'I've got some advice: Don't do it!'

She blamed Gazza for taking her ex-husband out drinking. Nevertheless, she told UK Living: 'I am happy for them and I hope they make a go of it. But it would be against all odds because they have had such a stormy relationship.'

On the eve of the wedding, Colin Kyle begged his ex, Sheryl, to let him visit his son, whom he hadn't seen for three years. Meanwhile Gazza's limo service was working overtime, taking the couple to ZAH hairdressers in Stanmore, Middlesex, where they both had their hair bleached blonde and cut. The following day, a Cadillac picked up Sheryl from her home, while Gazza jumped in from a nearby street to avoid reporters. When the car hit heavy traffic in London's Marylebone Road, Gazza called the police to halt the media convoy pursing them.

Gazza's mum Carol was also out on a shopping trip to find a suitable wedding present and shared her purchases with the media, including what was on the price tag. She bought them a forty-four-piece silver-plated cutlery set for £472, a set of six silver wine goblets at £50 a pair and four matching napkin rings costing £19.95 each. As a treat, Carol was invited along to Gazza's surprisingly sedate stag night, watching the Euro '96 final a private suite in the Swallow Hotel in Waltham Abbey. His mates were told to bring their wives along.

Gazza took time off to give the *Sun* an exclusive about how much he enjoyed being a dad. He also said that he may play abroad again so that Sheryl and the family could find peace and quiet. He was, he said, 'fed up with all the hassle'.

Sheryl insisted that Gazza picked his brother Carl to be his best man over his ever-present oldest pal, sixteen-stone builder Jimmy 'Five Bellies' who she not unfairly blamed for attending some of his worst boozing binges. Carl was kitted out with an embroidered silk suit, identical to his brother's. A smaller version was made for Regan.

In all Gazza spent £4,000 on suits for the wedding. He insisted on buying a hand-made silk suit from the same tailors for Sheryl's father, Richard. He also had a silk suit made for seven-year-old Mason. And he paid for a dress for ten-year-old Bianca and Sheryl's pink silk wedding dress, along with matching pink satin shoes, covered in lace, by Jimmy Choo, costing £275. His other contributions to the wedding reflected his loyalty to Rangers—Scottish salmon and steak, and a pipe band from Barra.

The wedding day began with breakfast at the nearby Feathers hotel. Early in the morning, Gazza arrived stripped to the waist with a towel around his shoulders, having been for a dip.

At midday, seven white stretch limos with tinted windows pulled up outside. The guests piled in, but Gazza gave reporters the slip by the back way and making his escape in a Fiat Punto, though he then switched to a thirty-two-feet Lincoln Continental with a mirrored ceiling to join the monster motorcade, arriving at the venue swigging champagne. The thirty-five police officers on duty were said to be there to control traffic on surrounding roads, while sixty security men scoured the grounds of Hanbury Manor to keep intruders out, though they could not prevent photographers from rival publications circling overhead in helicopters.

Other hotel guests had been flung out half-an-hour earlier, though a small crowd of well-wishers hung about outside in the rain. One staff member said: 'There's been more security here today than when Princess Anne visited.'

Inside Hanbury Manor Sheryl had taken over the hotel's hair salon, bringing in her own people. Harry Anastasi and his creative team from the salon Zah spent hours arranging Sheryl's long blonde hair into an ornate style and even revamped Gazza's bleached blonde crop. Isabell Kristensen and her assistant were there to make sure there were no hitches with the dress.

At 2pm, the couple were married in the sumptuous Zodiac Room—a white, wood-panelled room with bas relief designs, a vaulted ceiling and the twelve signs of the zodiac on the walls. His face lit up when she swept down the grand staircase.

Inevitably the famously lachrymose Gazza was moved to tears by the moment and cried when he said: 'I do.'

Twenty minutes later they were in the bar. At three, they moved on to the medieval banqueting hall where a feast was laid on by Albert Roux, from La Gavroche. The menu included a carpaccio of smoked chicken, roasted Scottish salmon with asparagus and a mille-feuille dessert of summer berries—plus an extra-time slice of the three-tier cake—all washed down with vintage champagne.

At the reception Gazza turned on the tears again when he asked guests: 'Doesn't my wife look fantastic?' He glugged back a glass of wine to both stifle his sobs and fortify himself and blubbed: 'I love you all—but not as much as I love my Sheryl.'

Sheryl herself fought back tears when her daughter Bianca made a speech calling Gazza 'dad'.

'I think my mum and dad look lovely together,' she

said. She was wearing a dress like her mum, while her brother Mason wore a cream page-boy suit.

Chris Evans called for three cheers to the bride and groom who hit the dance floor as soon as they finished posing for *Hello!* magazine. To start the dancing, Sheryl chose 'Unchained Melody' by the Righteous Brothers, while Gazza followed it with Van Morrison's 'Have I Told You Lately That I Love you'.

Gazza gently placed a hand on his wife's waist for a romantic waltz which left their celebrity guests and family stunned. The groom then reduced guests to tears of laughter by breaking into a Michael Jackson-style moonwalk. By midnight, the couple were swept away by a limo and fell asleep in each other's arms on their way to another hotel, foregoing the £400-a-night bridal suite at Hanbury Manor. *The Times* said that the wedding was more Hollywood than Hertfordshire.

The excess of Sheryl and Gazza's do set a trend for hotel weddings. Their celebrations even edged the impending divorce of Charles and Di off the front pages.

Next stop was Heathrow where Gazza kicked a photographer's ankle when he got too close and Sheryl hid her ring under her sleeve. The couples' two-week honeymoon was spent in Hawaii, accompanied by staff from *Hello!* They stayed in a £1,500-a-night suite in the Grand Wailea Resort on Maui, where Sheryl was asked: 'It must be daunting marrying a legend?

'Yes,' she said and added romantically, 'But I entered into it with good faith. Unconditionally. You know when Paul knelt down on his good knee and asked for my hand, I said: "My hand? Silly boy, you can have the lot."'

Gazza said sagely: 'I'm glad we didn't get married earlier because we'd have been divorced by now.'

He also said he was not too impressed by the hotel and wished 'Five Bellies' was there—to manage security at least.

'I know it ought to be a time for me and Shaz to be alone, but it's raining,' he said. 'After a bit of chat and that, all I've got is me thumb to suck. With "Five Bellies", he's always got a drink or a laugh going. It'd be like having Chubby Brown in the Garden of Eden, man.'

Sheryl remained silent on this sore point. She and Gazza spent most of their time in the room, avoiding the glare of the assembled reporters—those from the tabloids naturally speculating on what they were doing there. Gazza had not even been spotted in the bar.

'Everyone is amazed by his behaviour. He seems a changed man now he is married,' said another guest. 'They are obviously a honeymoon couple—you can tell them a mile off. Even their hair matches!'

The good behaviour did not last long. Gazza was soon being questioned by the police after he allegedly smashed a photographer over the head with a rock. He had pursued the camera man after spotting him while sunbathing with Sheryl. Gazza told his bride 'I wish we'd gone to bloody Majorca' and threatened to sue the photographer for invasion of privacy.

Gazza and Shazza had planned to splash out £10,000 to end their honeymoon in Inverlochy Castle, near Fort William. But the request for five suites for friends and security staff couldn't be accommodated as the plush hotel was fully booked.

Security had been beefed out because Sheryl had been at the centre of a stalker scare. A man had been following her nearly every day for six months. Gazza was so worried he'd installed surveillance cameras and also a security intercom system at their home. Sheryl said that the pest followed her when she took the kids to school and shopped in the supermarket.

'This guy is a right weirdo and Sheryl is really worried,' a friend worried to the press. 'He is obsessed with Sheryl and she's been so frightened that her dad has been staying with her when Paul is away.'

Gazza confronted the man. 'He just laughed and told me I couldn't touch him.' Gazza said. 'He's a little guy with glasses and has been hanging around the house for six months.'

When Gazza went to the police, they told him there was nothing they could do unless the man committed an offence. But Gazza had problems of his own.

His life had been threatened for miming playing a

flute—supposedly from an Orange marching band—on the field. He revealed that a Rangers' fan had said he would cut his throat in a Channel Four fly-on-the-wall documentary *Gazza's Coming Home*. The documentary also portrayed the deep depression he had suffered over the ups and downs of his private life with Sheryl that was playing out across the newspapers.

'I want people to know what fame is like,' Gazza said on the programme, going on to admit: 'When Sheryl told me she was pregnant and, you know, I really s*** my pants.'

He also discussed his private life with Sheryl on the phone with Ian Wright. The call was tapped, and a recording was offered to the *Daily Record* for £2,000. The police were called, and Gazza thanked the *Record* for not publishing details of his conversation.

Sheryl got another shock when Gazza turned up with dreadlocks. He had flown Harry Anastasi to Renfrewshire to give him a new look. But there were darker Sheryl headlines, too, that would relegate other news from the front pages.

Just fourteen weeks after their fairy-tale wedding, after a boozy night out, Gascoigne allegedly beat up Sheryl in their room in Scotland's Gleneagles Hotel, leaving her with a black eye and facial bruises. Every finger but one on her left hand was dislocated in the drunken assault, said the *Daily Mirror*, and she was pictured with her arm in a sling and her hand bandaged.

Despite the stylish atmosphere at the hotel, things had not gone well. Sheryl received a torrent of Gazza abuse over a candlelit dinner in the exclusive hotel's restaurant as he downed whiskey.

'Gazza was appalling,' said a fellow diner. 'The waiters looked very embarrassed because he became increasingly loud and abusive towards his wife. She looked very upset. It wasn't clear exactly what the problem was, but he just seemed to get worse and worse.'

Later yelling was heard from the couple's £680-a-night suite with the children asleep in the room next door. After the bust-up, Sheryl was driven to a private clinic to be X-rayed to make sure she had no other injuries. Rangers even sent a medic in an attempt to keep the clash secret.

Later, in his autobiography *Gazza: My Story*, the England professional admitted ruefully that he had continued his abuse of Sheryl: 'I headbutted her and threw her to the floor. Her finger was broken, so she was screaming in agony. I tried to click the finger back into place and that made her scream even more.' Yet, in the moment, he had remained in a quandary, 'What I had done was terrible and I knew it, but I couldn't bring myself to apologise.'

The following day he thought better of it and Gazza phoned her and begged her to take him back. Sheryl had only agreed to marry him after he vowed never to hurt her again. A friend staying at their new home in Kilbarchan volunteered: 'Paul and Sheryl are back together. They won't be coming back here to the house.'

They were thought to be staying at the plush Cameron House Hotel on the banks of Loch Lomond, discussing their future together as was nursing her injury.

In a cloak and dagger operation, Sheryl was smuggled out of the hotel through the tradesman's entrance and picked up by a friend in a black Range Rover to outwit the media. Another driver, behind the wheel of a high-powered Mercedes, swung his car across the road to stop journalists and photographers following. She later sought refuge with her mum and dad in Hertfordshire.

Women's editor of the *Daily Mirror* Mary Riddell thought that, if Sheryl stayed with Gazza, she had better get used to the beatings.

'She knew, long before her marriage, what kind of a husband she had picked, but she chose to disregard the evidence,' said Riddell. 'It is no use supposing there will not be a next time.'

Mirror sports-writer Nigel Clarke called for England—if not Rangers—to drop him.

'At best Gazza is a troubled man and I say in no fit state to play for his country,' he wrote. There were also calls to have him jailed as he ostensibly caused actual bodily harm.

Fellow footballer's wife Lorraine Merson offered support to her fellow WAG. After helping her husband Paul battle his addiction to drugs and booze, the mother of three was rewarded by him threatening to kill her during a blazing row. The £5-million Arsenal striker, who played for England alongside Gazza, screamed at her: 'All you've ever been to me is a pathetic little insect, crawling around my feet and getting in my way.'

'I admit I went ballistic and lost control,' he said full of remorse. 'It has scared me as much as Lorraine because I didn't think it could happen when I was sober' about the black mood that had overtaken him.

Lorraine, who suffered beatings while Merson was hooked on drink and drugs, said to the press: 'I couldn't believe the old monster was back. I can't cope with that anymore—I can't cope with the fear of him hitting me again.'

He had agreed to move out of their home in Chiswell Green, Hertfordshire. She also confessed: 'I'm very close to Sheryl and we've both been through the mill with our footballer husbands. Being married to a famous footballer can put pressure on a relationship and we've both been on the receiving end of violence.'

Twenty-eight-year-old Merson went berserk after Lorraine told him she had gone for a night out with the girls while he was away training with the England team.

'He made a cutting remark or two and seemed jealous that I'd been able to enjoy a night at a restaurant without having a drink,' she said recounting the moment. 'We started to argue, and I ended up telling him: 'Paul, you're just no fun anymore. You've let your recovery turn you into a bore.'

'I didn't mean to upset him, but I wanted to tell him how I felt. His only response was to say that I had just made his mind up for him and our marriage was finished.'

In anger, he said he was going to look for a new place straight away. 'After we put the kids to bed the old Paul started to come back,' Lorraine told the *Sun*. 'He began to look very scary then started saying over and over again: "You're nothing but a bitch".'

'He looked as mad as I'd ever seen him. I tried to stay cool even though fear was welling up inside me', she said about the tense moments that night.

It was doubly hard, she confessed. When Merson called her an insect it was 'like he stabbed me through the heart'.

'How dare he say that to me after everything I'd done for him,' she went on. 'I put up with violence, boozing, other women and gambling when he was an addict and shared all his pain as he recovered.

'I lost control and threw one of my shoes at him and instantly knew I was in big trouble. He came back at me looking like a maniac and chased me into the kitchen shouting that he was going to kill me.

'I ended up cowering against a kitchen unit. There was a crash and one of my shoes banged into a cupboard door inches from my head. I went straight up to bed and shut myself in the room hoping he would keep away.'

But it was no safe haven. 'The door flew open and he grabbed the first thing that came to hand and threw it at me. It turned out to be a can of hairspray which cracked into the wall above me. He stood over me as I lay shaking in bed and said: 'I'm going to make your life hell. You ain't seen nothing yet.'

They planned to seek counselling in the hope of saving their marriage after the sudden ugly surge of aggression between them.

Gazza then apologised at a press conference—not for beating Sheryl but for getting sent off and fined £30,000 for kicking Ajax defender Winston Bogarde, leading to a 4-1 defeat.

'I'm a disgrace,' he said.

Although he only made a passing reference to his 'domestic troubles', he sought help for his alcoholism from Beechy Colclough, a counsellor who had treated a number of celebrities for addictive illnesses, including Elton John and Michael Jackson.

Meanwhile, Sheryl had to suffer her private life becoming the stuff of football chants as the first WAG. In a match against Aberdeen, Dons fans chanted:

'Gazza beats his wife' and 'You're scum and you know you are.' Most of his own Rangers fans refused to join in chants of 'There's only one Paul Gascoigne'—even after he had scored.

Sheryl then poured her heart out to a friend who passed it on to the *People*. She said that Gazza would belch in Sheryl's face, poke her in the eyes and even kick her between the legs, celebrating as if he had scored a goal.

'I used to see what he did to her, but she never told me half of it,' she said. 'After last Sunday Sheryl told me some things that are almost too shocking to take in.'

On one occasion, Gazza went berserk in an Essex restaurant when a male diner smiled at Sheryl.

'The guy was passing the table and politely smiled at Sheryl,' the friend said. 'Paul immediately accused her of having an affair with the guy. He was screaming accusations at her in the middle of the restaurant. Then he dragged her kicking and screaming outside. He completely lost control. The man was like an animal.'

Sheryl would visit her friend night and day with disturbing tales of abuse. After another bruising encounter, Sheryl had said: 'He's punched me, he's kicked me, called me names—but I still love him. There's something about him that makes me stay. You'll never understand what it's like, but I just can't leave him. People must think I'm mad to stay after all he's done but I swear I'm not giving up on him.'

The friend listened sympathetically but counselled Sheryl that she must leave her husband.

'She would agree that it was the best thing to do but she never did it,' she observed. 'It was as if she was convinced that he would change, that he could get rid of the devils turning him into a monster. He made her laugh and he was great fun to be with but his obsession for Sheryl destroyed all that.'

His paranoid fear of losing her drove him almost insane with jealousy. He also believed that his life would be over if England dropped him, but manager Glen Hoddle stood by him and Rangers fans also forgave him after he had scored a series of goals.

Speaking on Gazza's behalf, the friend defended him to the *Daily Mirror* that the footballer lost his rag after Sheryl wound him up with jibes about his humble roots that provoked the aggressive side of his character.

'Sheryl knows that Paul's Achilles heel is his Geordie background and his family. She'd realise how much her taunts would hurt him,' they said. 'This doesn't excuse what happened. But it might go some way to explaining it.'

Gazza shared this sensitivity with his family and friends, some of whom had even considered boycotting his wedding because of Sheryl and their jet-set lifestyle. His pal said Gazza was happiest with his own kind.

A source close to Sheryl jumped to Sheryl's rescue and bit back, 'She thinks they stir Paul up, making out she's a gold digger who only wants his money. They think she looks down on them—that they're all stupid Geordies who drink too much and don't know what life is about, and that they're bad for Gazza.'

Giving Gazza's side of the story, his pal said back in their bedroom at Gleneagles Gazza lashed out in fury, catching her with a blow to the side of the head. It was a toxic mix of sentiment that had caused him to explode in a drink-fuelled rage. But Gazza insisted that was the only thing. The three dislocated fingers were caused by her falling awkwardly rather than fortunately.

Shery's pal was adamant though on this occasion: 'There's no chance of reconciliation. She still feels very hurt about what happened. She thought getting married would stop all this nonsense.'

Sheryl was then seen moving furniture back into her Hertfordshire house with her father who said: 'We have nothing to say.' After the attack at Gleneagles, she had moved out of their house in Renfrewshire and stopped wearing his wedding ring. Sheryl made no comment about her husband being selected for England once more.

In an emotional personal interview with the *News of the World*, Gazza revealed how he broke down with shame and remorse in front of Sheryl's shell-shocked children just hours after he had beaten their mum black and blue.

'I'm on trial with Sheryl, the children, England, Rangers and myself,' he said. 'I felt so low and ashamed of myself. I knew what was being said after I had beaten up Sheryl.... The beating will haunt me for the rest of my life.'

Speaking from her home at Stanstead Abbots, Sheryl filled in her side of the story: 'I am angry that people have said I was winding Paul up or taunting him about his background. As Paul now knows, his violent outbursts are not sparked by any argument. They just happen for no apparent reason. We are both trying to find out why so we can have a future together.'

He, too, condemned the story that he had been provoked by Sheryl pouring scorn on his Geordie family as 'blatant lies'.

'I never taunted his family. Never in a million years would I do that,' she said. 'Paul knows why he attacked me. I can't go into it but it wasn't over anything really—he just flipped.'

Then Gazza himself came out to speak and explain why he had head-butted Sheryl and to apologise publicly to Sheryl whom he had wronged and abused in private. 'I just flipped,' he said about himself. 'It's like a self-destruct button that can happen at any time. It certainly wasn't about Sheryl ridiculing my family. My problem has nothing to do with her. I'm to blame. Suddenly I go out of control and I've got to find out why.'

Gazza said about that moment in which he found himself that he couldn't even remember how long it went on for.

'Sheryl and I were having a really happy dinner and enjoying a great night' he said. 'I wasn't dead drunk, but I just flipped. I went wild. I didn't know what I was doing. When I was hitting her, I wasn't in control—that's the frightening thing.

'When she fell and dislocated her hand her screaming snapped me out of my rage. Immediately I collapsed in tears of regret, bawling my eyes out. I couldn't believe what I had done.'

Gazza acknowledged that the assault made a mockery of his marriage vow to Sheryl more than two years ago that he would never beat her up again.

'I promised her the last time it happened I'd never lay a finger on her again,' he said. Bowing to the inevitable, he added, 'But obviously I hadn't solved my problem and suddenly it reared up again when neither of us were expecting it. I knew then that I had to get help.…'

'In the past I seemed to hate everybody for no reason. I can't describe the rage inside me. I am getting counselling to sort my life out.'

After this public outpouring of humility and disgust with himself, it was then reported that Sheryl was going with him to counselling. However, doorstepped three weeks after the incident, she said: 'That's news to me. I haven't seen Paul since it happened. I'm not saying if we have spoken. He says he has been for counselling—but is it true?'

Gazza was begging for one more last chance, but Sheryl confided in friends: 'I can't take any more.'

However, she refused to make a complaint to the police, so Gazza would not be charged. His only punishment would be to be dropped by BBC from their Lottery show and vandals painted 'Wife beater' on the road outside his mansion. A fortune teller made things worse by telling that his marriage to Sheryl had been a mistake, the press reported. On the other hand, he accepted £20,000 to star in a video about soccer violence.

After just four-and-a-half weeks Gazza and Sheryl met up at her home. He begged her to forgive him and told her that he was in therapy to control his violent rages. The sentiment was rather undercut when he spotted a freelance photographer outside Sheryl's home. Cameraman Nick Stern claimed the star hurled a rock that struck him on the back of the neck.

Moments later, Gazza, once again calm, walked indoors and spent an hour locked in heart-to-heart talks with his wife. Sheryl, wearing a smart black trouser suit, later emerged with her stony-faced husband. The pair drove off in separate Mercedes but returned in Sheryl's car.

Sheryl refused to comment on the rapprochement.

'I'm not saying a word,' she said when asked. 'Paul's gone back to Scotland.'

Soon after the couple checked into the £308-a-night Tylney Hall Hotel in Rotherwick, Hampshire, with the kids, occupying two suites. They were seen sipping £8.50 cocktails at the bar and spent £130 on a bottle only of Corton Charlemagne Grand Cru.

'Mr Gascoigne appeared to enjoy the wine very much—and so he should have done at that price,' confided hotel staff when asked. 'There were no cross words exchanged. They spent a lot of time chatting quietly, but neither of them was animated.'

They spent time together in a secluded corner of the hotel's oak-panelled lounge and going for long walks in the sixty-acre grounds.

'He was walking slowly, often with his head down. Gazza looked like a man with the problems of the world on his shoulders,' said an onlooker.

'I don't think anyone dared suggest Mr Gascoigne and his wife should go near any bows and arrows,' quipped an insider at the hotel. Guests at the eighteenth-century hotel have included Richard Gere and ex-wife Cindy Crawford, and Sean Connery. Facilities included a sauna, tennis courts, croquet lawn, a snooker room, a golf course and an archery range.

They stayed the weekend without incident, paying the £1,200 bill in cash. The day after they checked out, the couple were photographed at their Hertfordshire home. When they returned to Renfrewshire, they were happy to pose exclusively for the *Daily Mirror* with baby Regan.

A week later the couple were staying in the five-star Hyde Park Hotel in London's Knightsbridge. He was spotted having a crafty ciggie, perhaps he was trying to steady his nerves.

After that the couple took Bianca and Mason to see the musical *Oliver* at the London Palladium. Despite playing the family man, Gazza swore at photographers as they walked to the car. A few days later they went to the premiere of *101 Dalmatians* at the Royal Albert Hall Gazza wore a dinner suit with black bow tie, while Sheryl was in a midnight blue Herve Leger gown. They posed for photos but did not speak before an unsmiling Sheryl led the children in for the screening.

Other stars in attendance included Glenn Close, who played as the evil hound-hunter Cruella De Vil, Hugh Laurie, Joely Richardson, Joan Plowright, Imogen Stubbs, Stephen Fry, Patsy Kensit and Kate Moss. After the two-hour screening, guests attended a champagne reception at the nearby Royal Geographical Society. This was a mistake. After guzzling champagne, Gazza was itching for a fight and began abusing *Sun* journalist Andy Coulson who had published a series of damaging articles about him.

'Apparently egged on by Sheryl, Gascoigne took his

dinner jacket off before approaching me in the VIP area,' said Coulson. Gazza then threatened to beat him up and 'take your f***ing head off'. A violent altercation was only prevented by the intervention of Ross Kemp.

Coulson went on to edit the *News of the World*, then David Cameron's director of communication, before being jailed for phone hacking.

For months, Gazza and Sheryl were not seen together and there were rumours that she had finally given him the big E. This forced Gazza's hand and he had to make a statement about his marriage to the media.

'I've just come back from a lovely relaxing weekend in London with Sheryl and the kids,' Gazza told the *Daily Mirror*. 'We went ten-pin bowling and had a meal. We all enjoyed ourselves…. By spending as much time with Sheryl and the kids as I can, in addition to the counselling, I'm determined to sort everything out.'

England manager Glenn Hoddle also assured the press that the Gascoigne's marriage was intact, though Sheryl, who never relished living in Scotland, remained at their house in Hertfordshire. Gazza was looking for a transfer to an English club to be near her.

However, when he travelled down to London for a night on the tiles with his pals Chris Evans and Danny Baker, Sheryl gave him the red card again in a press interview.

'I didn't even know he was in London until I read the papers,' she said from their Hertfordshire home. 'I'm not expecting him back here. He won't be coming here.'

Friends believed it finally all over between the two of them and that this WAG soap was about to close.

'Yes, it is true. Sheryl has given Paul the boot,' said one. She hadn't seen him for a month.

Another said mournfully: 'They are not talking. It's clear she is serious about this and has no plans to see him. It looks as if this time it's for keeps and she seems determined to take it all the way to the divorce courts.'

Asked about a split Sheryl, wearing satin trousers and a bright floral shirt, refused to be drawn into any confidences and would only say: 'I can't talk about that.'

The week-long boozing session got Gascoigne into other trouble. The police sought to question him about assaulting a young woman in Regent Street. He was cruising with his mates in a stretch limo when she said she saw Chris Evans' ginger hair appear out of the sunroof and she went over to tell him how much she enjoyed his radio show. Gazza allegedly learned out and slapped her. But it would turn out to be a misunderstanding.

Seemingly unconcerned, he took a holiday in New York. Staying at the £400-a-night Peninsula Hotel, off Fifth Avenue, he went on a seventy-two-hour St Patrick's Day drinking spree around Irish bars, dressed in black with matching sunglasses.

Rangers thought he was going there with Sheryl to patch things up. Drama quickly piled up when they discovered he was on his own to continue drinking and they said they, like Sheryl in the past, were keen to dump him. He fought back by dismissing the young woman who had complained about him slapping her as 'a money-grubbing bitch'.

'It's obvious she just wants to get cash,' he said. 'I've got no problem with the police this won't go anywhere.'

She responded that he was a 'coward and a bully'. Gazza claimed he only gave her an Eric Morecambe-style slap with both hands. In the end, she dropped charges in exchange for a face-to-face apology.

Alone with her children in Hertfordshire, Sheryl said she and Gascoigne hadn't spoken: 'I don't know where he is. The last I heard he was going to New York, but I have not spoken to him. I was told he was going out last Friday.'

Asked for the purpose of his trip, Sheryl vented to the interviewer: 'You tell me. I honestly don't know. I have not seen Paul since Regan's birthday on February 18. I am not expecting to be in touch with him either.'

After he flew into Heathrow, he immediately headed to Glasgow to face the music. Rangers fined him £30,000 and he issued a 732-word statement contritely apologising for past behaviour to Rangers, the club's supporters, the woman he had struck, and Sheryl and their three children. He hadn't seen her for a month.

The *News of the World* then announced that Sheryl planned to file for divorce on their first wedding anniversary—the earliest date possible—citing irreconcilable differences and unreasonable behaviour. She was aiming for a half-share of his £10 million fortune. Still suffering from an ankle injury that has stopped him playing, he was forced to rest up in a retreat near Rangers' stadium. He sought desperately to speak to his wife. From there, he made persistent and tearful late-night phone calls to Sheryl—until she changed the number to avoid talking to him. She said she would only communicate with him through her solicitors.

Gazza was deeply affected by the fact that his wife didn't want to talk to him. Even football couldn't cheer him up this time. He retired to the pub with Chris Evans to cry into his pint. They watched the England-Mexico match on the wide-screen TV in the Sir Richard Steele pub in Belsize Park, North London. Landlord Kirk McGrath said: 'Gazza had come away from the TV at half-time and was sitting on a ledge by the stairs with Chris. He was crying and quite definitely having an emotional moment. He didn't seem that bothered by the football.'

But Gazza was soon back on form—singing, swearing and trying to climb on the table to dance—in a top Scottish restaurant. The Champany Inn near Edinburgh, which boasted members of the Royal Family among its clients, had to close its bar after Gazz, 'Five Bellies' and another pal had run up a £900 booze bill. The total bill came to £1,390 bill which Gazza paid.

Sheryl bumped into Chris Evans at a launch party for the movie *Scream*, but he avoided an awkward moment in front of photographers by saying discreetly: 'Later.'

It seems that Evans played peacemaker between the star-crossed lovers whose ups and downs competed on the front pages with match results. Within two weeks, friends said that Gazza and Sheryl were going to make up after meeting three times. She then went to watch him play Motherwell at Ibrox. Afterwards, instead of going out on the town, they returned to his mansion in Renfrewshire where the kids were waiting.

Sheryl appeared with him at a Rangers' party a week later. Five days after that they were spotted leaving a London hotel by a photographer. Gazza couldn't but call him 'f***ing scum' before spitting in his face.

Again the apology followed by Gazza's expressions of true love had their effect and he was soon back with Sheryl in Stanstead Abbotts. A neighbour said he had been around all week and the couple looked very happy. Gazza conceded hopefully the *Sunday Mirror*: 'We've been together for the last four days. Are we getting back together? What do you think?'

They celebrated his thirtieth birthday with a game of croquet.

'It was the pair's first public outing together since rumours of a marriage split,' said the *Daily Mirror*.

There was also a birthday bash organised by their friends Ross Kemp and his fiancée Rebekah Wade, editor of the *News of the World*. Gazza turned up at Sheryl's in a twenty-eight-foot eight-seater limo costing £50 an hour. He was barefoot with his calf heavily bandaged from his injury in England's victory over South Africa. After re-emerging in a multi-coloured Moschino waistcoat and black trousers, he waited for her in the back seat. A couple of minutes later she appeared wearing an eye-catching turquoise mini-dress and matching jacket, clutching a present under her arm. Her mum was left to babysit.

It was love at first sight, again. That summer the couple took a holiday in Florida and the Caribbean with the children. Staying at the top Sandy Lane resort on Barbados, an onlooker said: 'Gazza seemed thrilled to be with her. They looked like a young couple in love.'

The second honeymoon was costing them £1,200 a night. As Gazza and Sheryl frolicked by the pool, one guest said they were 'either madly in love or Oscar-winning actors'.

Clearly this was not enough of a holiday for Sheryl to make up for all the heart-burn and pain. After they returned to Britain, she disobeyed his strict orders to stay at home by jetting off to Portugal. Friends predict Gazza would 'go ballistic' when he found out. He had recently halved Sheryl's allowance as a penalty for leaving him behind when she took their baby son, her two other children and her parents on holiday to Cyprus. A close friend of the couple revealed what they knew to the press: 'If Gazza knew about the trip, he'd go nuts.'

Gazza was back in Scotland renewing his contract with Rangers when Sheryl sneaked off to model clothes by Isabell Kristensen, Fergie's designer, for *Hello!* magazine.

A friend privately told the *Sunday Mirror*: 'Sheryl's gone to Portugal just to defy him. She knows there's a risk to it, but she's prepared to take that chance. When she took the family to Cyprus a couple of months ago, he cut her money by half.

'She's told all her friends she doesn't love him. She doesn't like anything about him. She runs him down all the time. The only way they can survive together is seeing each other every other weekend. They couldn't live together as proper man and wife. But she likes the high life—film premieres and being in the newspapers. Whatever she wants, he gets her.'

Later that year, the relationship settled down. While Sheryl rarely travelled up to Scotland, they holidayed together in America and he regularly visited her in Hertfordshire.

'Me and Sheryl are not a problem,' he said. 'If I get a day off, I can jump on a flight and be home in one hour fifty minutes.

He was also planning to go and play in the US. 'If everything is OK with my wife Sheryl, I might go over to America for a couple of years and enjoy my football there,' he said contentedly about their new-found marital bliss.

11
Wag Claws

Things may have been all right between Sheryl and Gazza, but David Beckham's girlfriend Victoria Adams—aka Posh Spice—took a swing at her. Covergirl for the November 1997 issue of *Tatler*, Posh said about the Queen of WAGs: 'Some reporter came round to our house and asked me about being a football wife—he was comparing me to Sheryl Gascoigne. I couldn't believe it. I don't intend to dye my hair blonde.'

She copied a leaf out of Sheryl's designer book though, refusing to move to Manchester to be with her man because it did not have trendy stores.

'There are not many nice shops in Manchester,' she said. 'No Prada and Gucci in Manchester.'

She also hinted that David may get a transfer to a club in Italy when the boutiques were better but said: 'Promise me you'll leave that out—I'll get such hate-mail from those Man U fans. I get enough as it is!'

While Sheryl would not go to Scotland, she did fly out to Rome with footballer's wives Claire Ince and

Debbie Wright to watch their husbands play Italy—and do some shopping. There was then talk of Gazza moving back to Spurs to be nearer Sheryl.

Meanwhile David Beckham headed for Turkey to see the Spice Girls' debut there.

When Spurs pulled out of the deal, Gazza turned for advice to England manager Glenn Hoddle who had recently split from Anne, his own wife of twenty years after the World Cup qualifier against Italy.

'Dumping my wife was the hardest thing I've ever done. My private life was in turmoil,' he said. 'It was my secret, something I carried alone in the preparation for the biggest match of my life to date.'

A born-again Christian, Hoddle left his wife their £350,000 home in Ascot and went on to marry Vanessa Colburn, staying with her for fifteen years. Nevertheless, Anne and their three children turned out to see England knocked out of the World Cup by Argentina the following year.

The mentoring did little good as Gazza soon received a five-match ban for urinating on a teammate during a training session. He was contrite.

'I could kick myself for some of the things I have done on and off the pitch,' he said, claiming he tried to stay out of the limelight. 'I try to keep things as private as possible for me and my family and that is very hard.'

While Gazza pledged to be Mr Clean, Sheryl hit the headlines for poaching a nanny from *Eastenders* star

Gillian Taylforth, who went on to star in *Footballers' Wives*. That role won her number forty-nine in Channel 4's poll for the 100 Greatest Sexy Moments; for having sex on a snooker table. She also made the front page by suing the *Sun* for libel when the newspaper said she had been cautioned by the police for performing fellatio on her lover, and later husband, Geoff Knights in a slip road off the A1 in their Range Rover. In the *Sun*'s defence, defence counsel, George Carman QC, entered into evidence a thirty-five-minute home video of Taylforth performing party tricks—'suggestively posing with a large sausage... graphically simulating masturbation with a wine bottle' and boasting to the camera, 'I give very good head.' The incident gave rise to the sarcastic term 'Taylforth Sausage'. When the *Sun* won, she collapsed and had to be taken from court in an ambulance.

Dismissing criticism of her poaching the nanny, Sheryl said: 'It's a silly situation. It's not as though I dragged her here by her hair.'

Sheryl and Gillian lived just a few miles apart, but they were not friends. The nanny moved from a house with one child to one with three children, so Sheryl would have more time for her career in part-time modelling. Otherwise the households had some similarities. Geoff Knight served a jail sentence after a fight in an Indian restaurant. Both couples were living apart at the time after Gillian had been seen with a black eye.

12
A Star is Born

All was not sweetness and light at the Gascoigne home either. By the end of the year, the *Sun* was reporting that Sheryl was secretly consulting divorce lawyers as she was 'totally fed up' with Gazza's behaviour over recent weeks. The matrimonial lawyers' first job was to work out the size of deal she could accept in a settlement to end their seventeen-month marriage. 'She has spoken about the divorce happening very soon. She has said it is all over,' a source in the know confided to the paper.

Gazza took his new bad fortune badly. With his marriage on the rocks, Gazza was taking a hip flask of brandy into the changing rooms before a match. Former model Sheryl, however, was rebuilding her career ready for a new independent life. She had recently made a catwalk comeback and also took a TV job filling in for presenter Jenny Powell for a fortnight on Sky *One's Live Six Show*. Programme bosses hoped she would stay on as a roving reporter and build a serious career in the media.

Unaware of his wife's professional moves on national TV, Gazza was in New York at the time with 'Five Bellies' and another mate. He was even being the good guy, giving eggs and bacon for breakfast and steak for dinner to a homeless Vietnam veteran outside his £300-a-night hotel. The food was served on the hotel's bone-china plates and Gazza brought the silverware, also giving the vagrant $20 to boot.

Returning to Britain, Gazza dodged court officials who tried to serve him with divorce papers. Bailiffs eventually served the papers on Gazza's Scottish lawyer instead. Sheryl was seeking a £5-million settlement out of the unhappy marriage. She was also taking a £150,000-a-year job as host on the TV gameshow *Pressure* to make ends meet.

Of her job she said: 'I am nervous. I could fall flat on my face but at least I will have tried something new.' A Sky TV insider said confidently: 'It's over between Sheryl and her husband. That's why she can start her own career.'

Meanwhile there were other problems in the world of WAGgery. Gazza's England teammate Matt Le Tissier walked out on his wife and childhood sweetheart Cathy, and their two children, for nineteen-year-old barmaid Angela Nabulsi, before settling with *Home and Away* and *Emmerdale* actress Emily Symons. Ex-wife Cathy then took off with Ian Nuttal, boss of the Cod

Whopper chip shop.

Sarah Curtis, the twenty-one-year-old lover of Chelsea and England player Michael Duberry, was revealed as a benefits cheat, claiming £81.80 a week despite moving in with the £6,000-a-week star after having his baby. They lived in a £250,000 house not far from other WAGs Sheryl Gascoigne and Victoria Beckham. Boxer Frank Bruno and Arsenal star Ian Wright attended their baby Kayci's christening bash.

Sheryl announced that she would not be spending Christmas with Gazza that year given that she was divorcing him. Backing timidly into the limelight, she said: 'I don't think it does any good to talk about these things as it gets messy. If I was asked what I want for Christmas I would say I want to be with my children.'

Having cut the Gordian knot, she was unfolding her own career wings. She was taking over from Judy Finnigan on ITV's *This Morning* while she was taking three months off to have a hysterectomy. A part was also being written for her in the comedy series *Men Behaving Badly*.

'This is Sheryl's big break. Not only may she get the chance to host a national telly show, but she will also appear in one of the UK's biggest telly series,' said an insider about Sheryl's new-found film-star status. 'A cameo in *Men Behaving Badly* is being written about her because Martin Clunes and Neil Morrissey think it would be fun.'

As it was, her performance was not as well received as Gazz's footwork. Columnist Carol Sarler said in the *People* said she had no discernible personality.

'Sheryl Gascoigne looks like a scrubber and acts like a fool—which is no doubt how she attracted a man like Paul Gascoigne in the first place,' Sarler said. 'Far from cashing in on her Gazza years, Sheryl should be shutting up and putting him behind her.'

In the camera rehearsals, Sheryl wore a see-through blouse revealing a black Wonderbra cradling her breasts.

'Sky Live should be ashamed and so should Sheryl Gascoigne,' said Carol. 'She should go home; stay there; bring up her children properly. And put some bloody clothes on.'

But Sheryl had dealt with worse. 'The interest is going to be there, so I might as well turn it around,' she said about her career launch as a media celebrity.

Gazza spent Christmas Day with Rangers manager Walter Smith and his family.

'It was so sad. He had no family to be with and no real pals around him. Instead he watched Walter and his family open presents,' a friend told the press about Gazz's Christmas agony. 'All he has ever really wanted is to be part of a family. He wanted Sheryl to be his wife, his future and it didn't work out. So, he spends Christmas with somebody else's family and tries to enjoy their happiness.'

In the New Year, Gazza finally accepted that his marriage was over and that no further apology could mend it. 'I'm getting divorced,' he said. 'She served the papers on me, but I'm feeling fine."

He refused to make any further comment. A friend said with sorrow: 'Now that he's got the divorce papers, it's worse than ever—and he's sadder than ever. He spends every night with a bunch of blokes drinking in bars and playing at being silly wee boys.'

According to Sheryl, the marriage had been a mistake she couldn't have seen coming. 'I have been in the limelight for the last seven years,' she said. 'I haven't had a choice about that, other than maybe I shouldn't have married Paul.'

After selling the house in Renfrewshire, Gazz moved back to a £6,000-a-month lodge at Cameron House Hotel on the banks of Loch Lomond. The multi-million pound timeshare complex had round-the-clock security patrols and the lodge boasted a sitting room, dining room, two large bedrooms, three bathrooms, a continental kitchen, a Jacuzzi and two saunas, while the facilities at the hotel itself included a pool, spa bath, steam room, gym, squash court, snooker room and a health and beauty suite. Michael Jackson, Clint Eastwood, Luciano Pavarotti, Cliff Richard, Cher, Bob Hoskins, Liam Gallagher, supermodel Kirsty Hume and numerous soccer stars had also all stayed there.

One intimate friend said it was a clean break with his turbulent past with Sheryl: 'He didn't just sell the house when he and Sheryl split up. He sold everything that he had bought for her and the family, because he knew it was all over. The boat was sold, cars were sold—anything that reminded him of home and family.'

The Fletcher speedboat he had bought for £20,000 was sold for £7,000. Gazza had been sharing the house with 'Five Bellies' who said: 'People must think Paul and I are married. He goes out to training and I do the dishes. He gets home and I make the tea.'

The *Sun* then revealed in an exclusive the hell Sheryl had gone through with him. He tried to control what clothes she wore, when she could see her family and banned her from going out in case she met other men—and went mad when the ex-model agreed to do a charity photo-shoot, ordering her not to flaunt herself in front of the cameras.

His insane jealousy, along with his boozing and violent ways, drove their marriage to breaking point as she revealed the finest of the marriage on the rocks.

'Paul was always proud of Sheryl's stunning looks. But as their relationship broke down, he grew insanely jealous—her looks almost became a threat to him,' a close friend told the newspaper about what drove the footballer to his behaviour. 'He wanted a say in every-thing she did, even down to her choice of clothes. Last year she told him she had agreed to a celebrity shoot to help a favourite charity, hoping he would support her. Instead he went potty and told her he wouldn't allow it. He was ranting and raving that he wouldn't have his wife parading her body in front of the cameras. Sheryl used to be a model, for God's sake! Paul reacted like a stern Victorian husband rather than a 1990s man.'

The source said: 'He tried to vet her relationships with family and friends and didn't like her socialising without him. Time and again he wanted to stop her going out with pals because she might be around other men. Most of the time the only blokes she saw were her friends' other halves, but that made no difference.'

When bullying failed Gascoigne would cut Sheryl's cash to make her do what he wanted. He cut her monthly allowance from £8,000 to £6,000 after she left their home in Renfrewshire and returned to Hertfordshire with the children in 1996. Later he cut her allowance to £3,000 and took away a car he provided for Sheryl's nanny to use.

'He tried to use money to assert his authority, constantly warning her he would cut her spending if she defied him,' the source said. 'His domineering even extended to the kids. He would threaten to cut all ties with them unless Sheryl let him see them whenever he wanted—no matter how difficult it was. But when she made arrangements for him to see them, he often just didn't bother to turn up. Paul had a bizarre idea of what 'give and take' means in a marriage. He wanted Sheryl to give in to his demands or he would take things away from her and the kids.'

Another friend said: 'Once Sheryl had filed for divorce, she wanted to draw a line under all the misery. She had never spoken openly about how bizarre and terrifying Gazza's behaviour became. Now she is rebuilding her own life and a new career in TV and finally has some freedom. It must be as if a great burden has been lifted from her shoulders.'

The newspaper then revealed that Gazza had claimed that he had been possessed by five evil spirits when he beat her up—'and it's not gin, whisky, rum, brandy and vodka'.

One of Sheryl's friends gossiped to the *Sun*: 'Paul never once told Sheryl he was sorry or did anything to convince her he would change. He pulled out of sessions with a counsellor, but he happily visited a faith healer—and came back full of nonsense about demons. He told Sheryl this person had discovered he had evil spirits inside him. He claimed they were responsible for the attack, not him, but had now left his body—as if that made it OK. It was a pathetic excuse which proved to Sheryl just how lightly he was treating the whole incident.'

One of his friends said: 'He's now living in a hotel and spends his nights drinking with a bunch of blokes. Gazza has lost the things he really needs—marriage and a stable family life.'

There was barely a boozer in Glasgow that didn't boast a 'Gazza's Big Night Out' story from the regulars.

His friend continued: 'He is incredibly generous. He buys his round then gets the next one as well because he knows the rest of the lads can't compete with his income. It doesn't fit in with his bad boy image but he's just an ordinary bloke who takes a beer and wants to be married with kids. Unfortunately, he's got a talent for football and so he is treated like a superstar.'

Gazza was determined his son would never want for anything, but his generosity did no longer extend to Sheryl.

'Regan is his pride and joy, but Gazza is no mug. He is determined he won't be robbed,' said his friend about Gazz's thoughts. 'He told me 'That's the way it goes. The wife wants everything. But I'll give her only what she is entitled to and that's it'.'

He had already bought twenty-two-month-old Regan the personalised number plate R111GAN. It was on his new £75,000 Jaguar XK8 which he planned to give to his son when he learnt to drive. Even so, Sheryl had barred Gazza from taking Regan to Scotland after the death threats from Republicans.

Meanwhile Sheryl's TV career took off. She would miss the children though while they were looked after by the nanny.

'They are the most important thing in the world to

me,' she told the *Sun*. 'It's a joy being a mum. It's twenty-four hours, seven days a week non-stop but it's worth it. I wouldn't call it hard work, but it is a worry at times.'

When she was asked to stand in for Jenny Powell on Sky One's *Live Six Show* she had turned to Bianca and Mason for advice.

'I asked them what they thought and they both said, "Do it mum, do it—you'll be great!"' she said. 'They are loving every minute of me being on TV. All their school friends talk about it, so for them it's great. But I tell them I couldn't do it week in, week out, month after month. I don't see it as long-term and I'm lucky it's not a daily show.'

She was particularly concerned about leaving Regan.

'I've never left them before,' she said. 'Regan has an excellent nanny. She takes him out and makes sure he's doing things. So, I know he's not missing out, but I suppose I feel I am. He's probably glad to be rid of mum for a while!'

Speaking at the Shepherds Bush pub in west London that doubled up as the *Live Six* set, Sheryl went on: 'As soon as I get home and on the days I'm not working I like to devote myself to the three of them. It just means doing fewer things for myself. I will cancel a hair appointment or not go to the gym. I suppose I'm always trying to make it up to them for being away.

'Bianca's really growing up now and getting interested in clothes and things. She borrows my tops and I absolutely love it—we are great friends.'

Sky bosses were said to have been impressed by Sheryl who was taking her own new stellar career as seriously as Gazz was about football.

'People who don't even know me are ready to criticise so I want to be as good as I possibly can,' she said. 'I watch my shows and if I see myself doing something like fiddling with my hair, I stop it the next time. I hope each time I am on TV I am improving. I want to be judged on my performance. That way I can sit back and say, 'Well, you gave it your best shot.' If I'm no good, at least I tried.'

However, she wouldn't commit to any long-term project that would keep her away from home.

'It is the children who are the most important thing in the world to me, not a career,' she said. 'I think if you asked, they'd say I was the most important person to them, except perhaps All Saints for Bianca and Arsenal for Mason.'

She doubted that she would ever marry again, telling *OK!* magazine that she cannot imagine anyone wanting to take on her children and the baggage of her turbulent years with Gazza. But Sheryl said she was happier than she has been for years.

Things began to turn nasty when a private investigator offered to dish the dirt on Sheryl for £20,000—

if there was any. He approached Gazza's agent Len Lazarus who entered into negotiations. Nothing came of it.

However, the newspapers soon had the dirt on Gazza. The *People* reported on a kiss-and-tell affair: 'Gazza, 30, is scoring with married pub boss Irene Dunford, 52—a blonde who looks amazingly like his estranged wife Sheryl, only older.'

The assignation was taking place in Chris Evans' Notting Hill home.

'Irene has given Gazza ten out of ten for his performance between the sheets,' the story continued. 'She claims he can make love up to five times a night and can keep going for more than three hours.'

The affair began when she sent him a nude photo of herself in the bath along with her phone number. She said Gazza thought she was thirty-five.

'We spoke to each other on the phone for months before we met,' she said. 'He was very, very upset about his marriage break-up and I was concerned about his drinking. He didn't want all the hassle of the divorce from Sheryl and the money and everything. I told him to get back with her and stamp out the drinking all together. I didn't want him to become another George Best.'

The *People* had a tape of a phone call. On it, Irene said: 'He's just fantastic looking. He's nothing like the pictures. He's ten-and-a-half stone of pure muscle.'

And she related how he had kissed her goodbye on the doorstep naked.

'I've had to tell him he's going to give me a heart attack twice. I've had to tell him to lay off,' she said.

Irene, a former glamour model who ran the Rat and Carrot bar in Chelsea, would sneak out for three or four hours, telling her husband she was seeing a woman friend. Gazza even talked about putting money into her bar, which had been a hangout for George Best. She claimed that Best had been a lover, along with Frank Sinatra and the Marquess of Bath.

Her fifty-seven-year-old husband Melvyn said: 'I'm not at all angry with her. She's been a good mother to my children. But I'll warn her—I could find myself a twenty-three-year-old netball player next.'

Gazza was angry when she spent £8,500 on a facelift which didn't change her appearance. He dropped her after he was left on the bench for a match where England was beaten by Chile. He wasn't even drunk, she complained. She said she thought that Gazza was looking for a younger model, someone famous—perhaps one of the All Saints.

Sheryl was not surprised about what was taking place as Gazza had been spending time in London.

'I know he has been spending a lot of time down here, but I don't know where or why,' she said. 'Apparently he's going round denying it—which he would.'

The *Daily Record* pointed out, cruelly, that Irene was old enough to be his mother.

As Sheryl predicted Gazza denied the affair with the former Page 3 girl Irene, saying it was a 'pack of lies'. However, he did admit to phoning her after the nude photo had arrived.

'I told her to ring my dad instead,' Gazza said about what had happened. 'I showed it to the Rangers lads and my dad. I told my dad to take her out, but he wasn't interested and told me, 'Neither should you be."

But 'Five Bellies' had invited Irene to a party at Chris Evans' house.

'She told me she'd had loads of affairs, but her husband didn't mind because she was the boss,' Gazza said. 'I thanked her for the letter and had a chat about football and that was it. I didn't sleep with her.'

An All Saints track had been playing during this conversation and she suddenly accused him of wanting them.

'It was mad,' he said. 'I've not slept with All Saints, I just like their music.'

Evan's girlfriend Suzi Aplin then thanked her and showed her to the door.

'I forgot all about it because I was going through a hard time with the divorce and crying every night,' said Gazza. 'Chris was comforting me about that and said, 'Be careful with that woman.' Suzi also told me to be careful with her because she seemed obsessed with

Sheryl.

'She was saying terrible things about Sheryl and me. She told me she'd just had an eye operation and one of her eyes was black and she was coming round to see me. I said, 'If you come round here, you'll have another black eye.''

Gazza then told the *Sun* that he had not had sex for five months.

'I'm celibate because I still love Sheryl,' he said. 'I'm not a guy who sleeps around, especially as I'm going through a divorce. I've not slept with anyone for a long, long time.'

A woman like Irene held no interest for him.

'All I'm interested in is football, Sheryl and my kids,' he said. 'I'm heartbroken by this. It will upset my wife and children and will affect my football for Rangers and England.'

Gazza said, as a result of the story, he could not see Regan on his second birthday. Irene then phoned him in Scotland to say that she had been ratted on by a female friend that she had confided in.

'I will wring her f***ing neck,' he said. He told her to deny everything. That's what he had done. Adding: 'I hate all the f***ing women in the f***ing world.'

She then explained how the incriminating tape had been obtained by *People*. 'They can have the f***ing tape, I couldn't care less,' said Gazza.

What he did not realise was that that conversation

was being taped too. A full transcript appeared in the *Daily Mirror* with expletives deleted.

Gazza was soon seen knocking back the pints and was dropped from the Scottish Cup replay against Motherwell. Soon he had been sold to Middlesbrough in a deal that would bring him £30,000 a week for the next three years.

13
Wag's End

Then the impossible happened. Gazza and Sheryl were seen out with the kids at the charity premiere of *Mouse Hunt* starring Lee Evans. Gazza swore at photographers before storming off. But he later relented and stood smiling with Sheryl and the children for a picture. They refused to comment on whether they were getting back together.

Daily Mirror showbiz reporter Polly Graham asked: 'Mr Gascoigne, are you and Sheryl reconciled?'

He replied: 'F*** off, you silly fat cow.'

The children looked shocked while Sheryl merely looked blank.

'I'm just here to enjoy the film,' he told other reporters.

Their reconciliation stunned other celebrity guests including Jonathan Ross, comedian Alan Davies and TV chef Gary Rhodes.

'They looked very relaxed and without a care in the world,' said one onlooker.

'Paul was going to take the kids on his own but then Sheryl decided she wanted to go too,' said a spokesman for the footballer. 'It doesn't mean there is any change in their relationship.'

Within a month, he told *The Times* that he was still hoping for a reconciliation with Sheryl. And he was seeing ghosts.

In an interview with Danny Baker, he admitted that if he had married someone with whom he'd grown up and gone to school with, it might have all worked out better. Someone prepared to sacrifice her entire personality for him might have been able to cope.

Gascoigne and Sheryl did still talk—and she still dressed him in designer clothes.

'I'll always work to get back together again,' he said. 'I always wanted to be a professional footballer and to have a good marriage.'

The *Daily Record*'s Joan Burnie said: 'To Gascoigne, Sheryl was the perfect partner—the model, the trophy wife.... Like a child, Gascoigne needs nurturing. Women, like managers, are expected to provide this comfort—no matter how often he lets them down.... Part of the problem is that Gazza has been infantilised. Football has kept him a boy.'

Yet the papers had a blow in store. It was not long before they were reporting that Sheryl had a new man in her life—twenty-six-year-old Birmingham rugby player Gavin Batey. They met at a charity fashion show at a hotel in Coventry where he was modelling, and Sheryl was *compère*. In one sequence she played a bride and he dressed as a groom.

'Gavin was really serious about Sheryl almost from the start,' a friend said. 'They hit it off straightaway. He took her number and called her. Pretty soon they were calling each other every day. Gavin is very tall, fit and handsome and a bit of a lady-killer. He has loads of girlfriends.

'He's a rugby lad and you'd have expected him to be boasting he was dating Sheryl. Instead, he kept it dead quiet and told only three of his closest friends. That shows how serious he was.

'He wanted to date Sheryl straight away, but she explained to him that Paul made life really difficult for her, keeping tabs on everything she does. Paul wants to know who she's seeing and even what clothes she wears. But she really liked Gavin and was determined to find a way to spend time with him.'

They spent the Bank Holiday weekend together. She told Gazza and friends that she was off to the Monaco Grand Prix. Instead she and Gavin spent four nights in Birmingham's posh Hyatt Hotel where world leaders stayed during the G8 summit the week before.

'Gavin's absolutely gorgeous but most importantly he makes Sheryl laugh and has brought a smile back to her face,' said a friend. 'When they met, Sheryl was extremely depressed. He's made her see life in a more positive light. Neither Gavin nor Sheryl are looking for a serious relationship at the moment. Sheryl is still going through a traumatic divorce and Gavin has just been a great pal.'

Ex-Royal Marine Batey was working as a forklift truck driver. He ordered flowers to be waiting for Sheryl in her suite. He also borrowed his boss's Mercedes for the duration. They used the hotel's service lift so that Sheryl would not be recognised going in and out of the main entrance.

On the Saturday night, the couple shared a romantic dinner at a seafood restaurant in Hockley. On Sunday, Gavin was in Sheryl's suite and the couple were not seen out all day. That evening, they went to the Chung Ying Gardens in Birmingham's Chinatown district. On Monday they went out for a drink with his best friends to a village pub south of Birmingham. They spent most of the next day together at the hotel before Sheryl drove back to her home at Stanstead Abbots.

The friend said: 'He says Sheryl's something special—but they are taking things slowly. It's not a big romance, more a friendship, but who knows what will happen.'

The couple got on so well they planned another getaway break while Gazza was away on at the World Cup duty. But then he was dropped from England's World Cup squad. There were reports that he had got drunk at a karaoke party and was thought to have been smoking heavily. The last man out of the bar, he had to be helped to his room by his teammates.

Sheryl phoned Batey and said she thought that news of their relationship had affected Gazza's performance while he was in Spain making his final attempt to get in the England squad. She said Paul was unable to concentrate and it would be impossible for her to see him again while Gazza was in the country.

It was Sheryl Gazza ran to when he was dropped. He turned up in Stanstead Abbots wearing his England tracksuit and refused to speak to the media as he rushed inside.

'Don't ring the bell. Don't try to knock on the door,' he told reporters.

The following morning behind tightly drawn curtains and blinds he gave an exclusive interview to Rebekah Wade where he admitted he had been drunk at training and had flown home to Sheryl for help.

'She has been fantastic,' Gazza told the press warmly about his ex. 'She has told me to pick myself up and not let it get me down. Hard words, but she's right.'

He emerged wearing a bright orange sports top and blue tracksuit bottoms. Stepping briskly from the house, he got into the driver's seat of a red Range Rover.

Seconds earlier, Sheryl had carried two-year-old Regan out to the placed him in a child's safety seat. But why was she so forgiving? The *Daily Mirror* said: 'It's because years ago, when she was a struggling and starving single mother, she discovered food parcels left on her doorstep every day. The donor? None other than Gascoigne himself.'

The paper also said that Gazza had flown home from the England training camp in La Manga near Alicante, Spain, leaving his luggage behind, because he had heard that she was seeing another man.

'Sheryl told him that Paul was terribly upset that she'd been seeing someone else and that instead of concentrating on making the squad he'd been distracted,' a friend of Batey said. 'She apologised but said Paul would be keeping an even closer eye on her now and another meeting couldn't be arranged for the time being. But she promised to phone Gavin and keep in touch. Sheryl told him she had really enjoyed her brief stay with him in Birmingham. He told her he really liked her and had found her a lot of fun.'

In the past Batey had been one for quick, short-term relationships, but it seems he wanted this one to last.

'He's upset now that Paul is back, and their plans are smashed. Everything is on hold. Gavin is also worried that Paul will try to patch up his marriage and win Sheryl back,' the friend continued.

However, former girlfriend Zoe Higton warned Sheryl that, like Gazza, Batey could be a boozy clown.

'He likes his sex, his beer and his women,' she said. 'But he has no real depth. He's not the sharpest pencil in the box.'

Sheryl, Gazza and Regan went to have lunch together at Hanbury Manor, the exclusive hotel where they had married, while the police guarded their home. Later Gazza explained: 'I came home to Sheryl because out of anyone in the world she knows me the best. When I am in a state like this, she is the only person that can handle me and that's why I came here.'

The couple then flew out with the kids to Miami. Sheryl wore a sleeveless black T-shirt with skin-tight beige leggings, Gazza a blue casual jacket, blue checked shirt and jeans. They waited for forty-five minutes in the VIP before a buggy took them to the departure lounge. Holding a brown leather holdall, Gazza sat on the back seat between Sheryl and Bianca.

While Sheryl sunbathed in a silver bikini, she shared a kiss with Gazza who was looking a little chubby in his black swimming shorts. Journalists observed other tender scenes between him and the kids.

A fellow holidaymaker said: 'They looked very happy together, just like any couple enjoying each other's company on holiday with their kids.'

Rooms in their five-star hotel on the millionaires' paradise of Palm Beach Island cost up to £2,000 a night. Gazza and his party are staying on the fourth floor, accessible only by special key and had its own private check-in desk and concierge. The holiday was paid for by Gazza's £50,000 payoff from England for helping them get into the finals. They would be joined there by the Spice Girls who were starting a tour.

While the *Sunday Mirror* speculated whether their tender kiss signified a rekindled romance or even reconciliation, it also reported that Sheryl had told her lawyers she wants half Gazza's fortune, then estimated at £16 million.

An intimate friend told the newspaper: 'Sheryl is going for gold. She doesn't think she's being greedy. She has put up with hell during her marriage to Paul and she has got their son Regan to think of.

'She sacrificed her modelling and TV career for Paul. She put everything on hold while he went out and earned a living. It's only now, after their separation, that she's been able to work. Gazza was such a handful she could never do it before.'

Now it was her turn.

'She's always been there for Gazza when things have gone wrong, to clean up the mess. And now it's no different. Sheryl's still his shoulder to cry on. She's a very family orientated person and she understands that Paul needs her now more than any time in his life. That's a measure of her strength and kindness—but as far as romance is concerned it's definitely off the cards.'

The friend said that Gazza was simply playing to the cameras with the kiss on the beach. He wanted the show the world that there was still hope of saving their marriage, when the harsh reality was that Sheryl was determined to go ahead with the divorce. She was looking for a bigger house near her current home in Hertfordshire and she had been offered a new show following the success of her chat show on satellite TV.

However, the waters were muddied when the *Sun* reported that he was seen stroking Sheryl's breast, then peeked down his swimming trunks with a smile. The headline read: 'Gazza grabs Shezza then checks his tackle.'

The story went on: 'The disgraced ex-England soccer ace appeared to have won back her heart as she let him caress her in full view of their children, photographers and guests at their holiday hotel. Sheryl, 33, giggled—then gently moved his hand onto her tanned tummy. Grinning Gazza, 31, nestled his head on her shapely chest and held her hand.'

The following day, they were seen sunbathing together instead of watching England's first World Cup knock-out victory against Tunisia on the TV. An onlooker said: 'Gazza cut quite a sad figure having a kickaround on the beach with Sheryl's kids.'

After their holiday, Gazza was back to his old form arriving back at Gatwick with Sheryl and the kids. He swore at photographers and had a run-in with officials who stopped him when he tried to nip through customs without his bags. Sheryl did not look happy to be home either.

Nevertheless, Sheryl and Gazza's quickie divorce was still going ahead. Within a month, the decree nisi was rubber stamped in London's High Court and a full-blown decree absolute would follow six weeks later. Sheryl was granted custody of Regan and a £1-million-plus settlement. This included a lump sum of £700,000 and £120,000 a year to support herself and the kids. She also kept the couple's £300,000 home in Hertfordshire, a £45,000 Jaguar car, a £40,000 Range Rover and expensive jewellery. She had reportedly been asking for £5 million.

'The holiday was a last-ditch attempt to save their marriage. But two weeks after they got back Sheryl lodged the papers when it became obvious his behaviour hadn't changed,' a close friend said about the revolving-door relationship of the lovers. Sheryl was heading for the exit, though, 'Sheryl still loves Gazza but simply can't live with him anymore. She has got to the end of her tether with his drinking and violent out-bursts. She wants to remain friends but doesn't want to be married to him.'

Sheryl herself issued a more unforgiving statement to the media for Gazza to read: 'I consider that Paul's behaviour has affected my health. I reserve the right to give further details should this become necessary in due course.'

The divorce was not contested. One of Gazza's

close friends spoke frankly: 'We feel very sorry for him because it is no secret he wanted desperately to repair the marriage. But we always believed that Sheryl was wrong for him—that she was just on a celebrity ego trip. We are glad she is out of his hair and that he can get on with his life.' Whether they knew their friend remained to be seen.

Gazza accused Glenn Hoddle of betraying the trust between player and manager after being dropped from the World Cup squad. In the forthcoming book *Glenn Hoddle: The 1998 World Cup Story*, Hoddle said Gascoigne was unprepared for the World Cup because he was 'constantly preoccupied' with his separation from his wife. The England manager described how the player spent hours on his mobile to his wife when he should have been resting before a match. Hoddle said Gascoigne was 'mentally all over the place'. Gazza smashed Hoddle's hotel room up, the manager said.

Adding insult to injury, Sheryl flew out for a holiday in La Manga in Spain—the very place Gazza had been dropped from the squad. Meanwhile Gazza was pole-axed by news that his friend, forty-three-year-old David Cheek, was found dead in his bedroom by 'Five Bellies'. They had all been out on a five-hour binge with Gazza.

Though divorced, Sheryl continued her career as a WAG as best she could, posing at a London show in an Isabell Kristensen dress to raise cash for the charity 'Goals for Addiction'.

Gazza's career also continued its decline with boots manufacturers withdrawing their sponsorship and him doing a *Full Monty* strip with four of his pals at a mate's wedding. He was seen crying at the railway station in Stevenage, Hertfordshire, tired and emotional. It was thought that he was making for Sheryl's home. Station staff said he was absolutely plastered after a four-day binge in Dublin involving a group of Swedish blondes. Friends feared he was having a nervous breakdown.

It was thought that Sheryl rescued him, picking him up and taking him to the nearby Hanbury Manor Hotel at Ware to sleep it off. Gazza was soon checked into the £2,000-a-week Priory Hospital in Southampton, where former England teammate Paul Merson had been treated. Experts warned Gazza grimly that he would be dead by forty if he carried on with alcohol abuse.

Gazza soon escaped and went on a fifteen-hour drinking binge. He did not play for England again and transferred from Middlesbrough to Everton in 2000. Two years later he moved to Burnley, Gansu Tianma in Japan and Boston United, then lasted a few weeks as manager of Kettering Town and has not worked in football since.

In 2006, he had a new girlfriend, twenty-nine-year-old single mother Jenny Wilkins. They met in a bar in Kensington and hit it off when they discovered they both came from Gateshead.

'He was so much fun, we'd go out to bars and he'd

order three or four bottles of Dom Perignon and we'd get drunk,' she said. 'We'd go to music bars where he'd ask me to get him cocaine. We smoked spliffs together.'

Gazza was no longer a footballer and Jenny had no aspirations to be a WAG.

'He kept pestering me to be his full-time girlfriend, but I refused because I was with someone else,' she said. 'Yes, we were more than friends and we did have sex, but I didn't ever class myself as his girlfriend. He'd pay me £100 just to sit with him in the casino. I'd get bored but he'd get angry if I said I wanted to leave.'

Soon there were signs that things were going very wrong with him.

'I'd pick him up in my Golf GTi and he'd sit in the back on my daughter's booster seat,' Jenny said. 'Then he'd sing Ray Charles's 'I've Got a Woman' at the top of his voice. It was very odd. He sat in that seat every time. Looking back, it was clear this was the beginning of his breakdown.'

His drinking was clearly out of control. Jenny claimed Gazza's day started with six strong whisky hot toddies. Then it was on to neat whisky, vodka and brandy.

'At night he liked to drink wine or Dom Perignon or Bollinger champagne. I once saw him drink for eighteen hours until he collapsed,' Jenny said. 'He went heavy on the drugs, too.'

He was also bulimic. She made him dinner at my

house once and he made himself throw up in the bathroom. There was blood everywhere.

While they were together, Gascoigne moved into the Lennox Hotel in Notting Hill because he hated being alone. In a safe in his room, he kept £72,000 and a £100,000 diamond necklace he had once given to Sheryl. He told her he'd sold it.

'He was obsessed with keeping the room neat and with washing his hands,' said Jenny. 'He had several showers in the day and would repeatedly flush the toilet.'

After her divorce, Sheryl's career as a TV presenter flourished. Among were credits were a stint on ITV's *Loose Women*. She appeared on *I'm a Celebrity...Get Me Out Of Here!* While Gazza was homeless, she lived in a £2-million house with a sauna, swimming pool, tennis courts and a cottage in the large grounds.

She was doing so well that in 2004 Gazza took her to court to slash her maintenance payments by half.

'It's hard for her,' said a friend. 'They aren't even on speaking terms. Now he is demanding Sheryl no longer use the Gascoigne name. But she is the mother of his son.'

In 2009, she published *Stronger: My Life Surviving Gazza*, an account of her marriage. Gazza's reaction to the book was published in the *News of the World* under the headline 'You Lying Bitch!' Sheryl sued for libel and won an unreserved apology from the newspaper and an undisclosed five-figure sum. She then piled grief on News International, owner of the *News of the World*, complaining to the Leverson Inquiry on phone hacking that the press had portrayed her as a gold-digger.

14
Long Live the Wags

Sheryl's role as victim was taken over by Ulrika Jonsson who was beaten up by her boyfriend footballer Stan Collymore. He punched and kicked her at a late-night party for Tartan Army fans at the Auld Alliance pub in Paris marking the beginning of the World Cup.

Scottish TV presenter Martin Geissler witnessed the attack.

'She was lying on the ground screaming and bar staff then grabbed Collymore and threw him out,' he said. 'He was in a real rage but came back later to make the peace but left alone a short while later. Ulrika left fifteen minutes later in a chauffeur-driven car.'

Barman Stephen Dixon said he had been shocked by the incident: 'I couldn't believe he would behave like that. We just grabbed him and got him out the door as quick as we could.'

Collymore's agent issued a statement saying: 'He is beside himself with remorse and made it clear to me he apologised immediately and subsequently to Ulrika and wishes to make that apology public.'

Collymore himself said: 'A stupid and silly argument had developed throughout the course of the day between myself and Ulrika, someone who I have realised for some time is very special to me. My actions were totally reprehensible, something I am not proud of and finding very difficult to come to terms with.'

Ms Jonsson, who was seen wearing dark glasses, issued her own statement saying: 'I would like everyone to know that I am fine, and I confirm that my relationship with Stan Collymore is now over.'

Like Sheryl, she refused to take the matter to the police. Previously she had stuck by him when he was accused of assaulting former girlfriend and mother of his child Michelle Green. He denied the accusation and was cleared of any charges in Cannock Magistrates' Court six weeks earlier.

Good to her word, Ulrika dropped Collymore and began dating German hotel manager Marcus Kempen. They broke up soon after she had his child in 2000. She went on to have an affair with England manager Sven-Göran Eriksson, who had an on-going relationship with Nancy Dell'Olio. She had followed him to England after managing Lazio.

A true WAG, Ulrika became a columnist on Rebekah Wade's *News of the World* where she regularly commented on Eriksson's personal life. Her column was dropped after he resigned as England manager.

Nancy Dell'Olio used her position as a WAG to host *Footballers' Cribs* on MTV where she gave viewers tours of the luxury homes of English football players. 'Nancy is a dream signing for us,' said series executive producer Sean Murphy. 'She's the first lady of football, so is in the perfect position to give us a real insider's view.'

She went on to launch a range of lingerie and appeared on *Strictly Come Dancing* and *Celebrity Big Brother*.

David Seaman married Debbie Rodgers at Castle Ashby in Northamptonshire. Although the wedding has been planned for months, Debbie still had to dash off to a nearby craft centre to buy two flower baskets for her little bridesmaids. Stallholder nineteen-year-old Liz Fitzjohn said: 'Debbie rushed in. She had obviously forgotten the baskets. She looked pretty and happy. The castle is a real fairy-tale place. They couldn't have picked a lovelier setting.'

Debbie wore an ivory satin wedding gown designed by Neil Cunningham, who made the bridal dress for Tory leader William Hague's wife Ffion. The couple had sold the story of their wedding and the photographs to *OK!* magazine for over £50,000. Even Gazza turned up with 'Five Bellies' and a woman—believed to be wife Sheryl—crouched in the back seat of his £60,000 Jaguar.

Meanwhile England manager Glenn Hoddle

invited the WAGs to join his squad at France '98—'To lift the players, not to have sex,' he said. Nor would he be imposing a sex ban if they reached the last sixteen. This may not have bothered Claire Ince, whose husband Paul said: 'My wife won't like this, but tackling is better than sex. I like the crunching sound.'

It was thought that the move would encourage more women to take an interest in football. The invitation was a far cry from the treatment of the wives and girlfriends at the 1966 World cup when they had to wait outside as the FA staged the celebration banquet at the Royal Lancaster Hotel in London following the historic 4-2 victory over West Germany. They were only allowed in once the meal had finished and the dancing had begun.

Wives and girlfriends were also flown out to Mexico before the 1986 World Cup. In Italy in 1990, Bobby Robson flew over the team's wives and girlfriends to the pre-tournament base in Sardinia. They flew home before the big kick-off but returned on a special day trip when England reached the semi-final against the Germans in Turin.

Mariana Le Saux, wife of left back Graeme, did not take up the offer, taking a holiday in the south of France instead because the England squad don't get days off during the World Cup and wives are encouraged to keep a distance.

'We're only allowed to see them for one day,' she

said. 'They want the players to concentrate and they think we'll distract them.'

Twenty-six-year-old Mariana complained of the role a WAG.

'You don't get weekends together, and you can't be spontaneous and just say 'Let's go away tonight!" she said. 'When Graeme left Blackburn for Chelsea, we went within two hours. He was on the phone saying 'Pack your bags, we're going to London tonight!"

She had just finished the examinations for her degree—not something usually expected of a foot-baller's wife.

'It takes one person, and that's it, you're all labelled,' she told *She* magazine.

Beatrice LeBeouf, wife of France's centre back Frank, concurred: 'When I saw the wives at Tottenham and Arsenal I understood why people think we're stupid and only good at showing our bottoms.'

Goalkeeper David Seaman planned to marry Debbie Rodgers after the end of the tournament. When he called to tell his son, who had just turned thirteen, he assumed his dad had called him to wish him Happy Birthday. Instead, according to his aunt, the boy said: 'You left us on my birthday, you put the house up for sale on my birthday, and now all this is going in the press on my birthday.'

There were, of course, these pitfalls to being a foot-baller's wife. When Dean Holdsworth had an affair and the girl spilt the beans, his wife Sam did not hold back. The woman, she said, was 'uglier than a Rottweiler'.

'She said Dean caressed her all night,' cried Mrs Holdsworth. 'I know Dean, and believe me, Dean does not do caressing. These days I see the young footballers' wives when their husbands get into the premier league. The think they know it all, I think: 'Watch out. He's coming home on time now, but a year down the line you'll be waiting for the phone to ring and you won't know where he is.'

There were other downsides. When Bournemouth went into receivership in 1997 the players were not paid. Steve Fletcher and his pregnant girlfriend Lynn Gibbons were trying to move house.

'The mortgage was put on hold for six weeks,' she said. 'The people we were buying from were livid. In the Premiership they're paid so much that these things aren't a concern, but we were thinking: 'What if he does lose his job?' I'd have to go straight back to work. We talk about what would happen if he's injured, or when he's too old. His father runs a pub, so we'll probably do that. It's very different now, but at the time we had no idea whether things would be alright.'

Then there was the ever-present danger of wannabe WAGs.

'There's always the same women hanging round the gates on a Saturday,' she said. 'If Steve was in the papers every time he talked to a girl I'd go mad.'

15
Empress of Wags

The first use of the term WAG—or WAGs—was in the *Sunday Telegraph* on 19 May 2002. It was reporting on the doings of Nancy Dell'Olio and the other womenfolk at the World Cup 'warm up' at the Jumeirah Beach Club in Dubai. She was trying to resolve her issues with Sven-Göran Eriksson after he admitted his affair with Ulrika Jonsson.

The newspaper said: 'It was never guaranteed that the wives and girlfriends (or 'the Wags', as staff at the Jumeirah Beach Club call them for short) would get along. Mrs Beckham's tongue, for one thing, has previously run away with itself: "Oo let the dogs out?" she is once said to have chanted at the glamour model Jordan, the on-off girlfriend of Dwight Yorke, one of her husband's teammates.'

Victoria Beckham—aka Posh Spice—became the archetypal WAG, though she was already famous before she entered the world of WAGgery. She had a successful career with the Spice Girls before she started dating David Beckham in 1997, going on to go solo, star in TV documentaries and running a fashion label. They first met at a charity football match. She attracted his attention by wearing a Manchester United strip for a Spice Girls' photoshoot. []

'I didn't really know who he was,' she said. 'I was never into football.'

He was shy and she instigated an exchange of phone numbers.

'I knew as soon as I met him that one of the most attractive things about David was that he shared the same sort of family values as me,' said Victoria. 'I really liked that.'

Posh and Becks soon became a media sensation, counting among their friends Elton John and Liz Hurley, who would become godparents to their first two children. He proposed to her on 24 January 1998 in a restaurant in Cheshunt, Hertfordshire.

The couple married in 1999 at Luttrellstown Castle in Ireland. Beckham's teammate Gary Neville was the best man, and the couple's infant son, Brooklyn, was the ring bearer. The Beckhams had an exclusive deal with *OK!* magazine, but newspapers were still able to obtain photographs showing them sitting on golden thrones. Over four-hundred staff were employed for the wedding reception which was estimated to have cost £500,000. They honeymooned in Andrew Lloyd-Webber's house at Cap Ferrat.

Unlike other WAGs, Posh earned more money than her husband and it was only in 2001, when Sven-Göran Eriksson made Beckham England's captain, that he became Britain's foremost sporting idol. —Given her prominence, when she turned out to support her husband as captain of the England team, she became *de facto* leader of the WAGs. They were tabloid royalty, living in 'Beckingham Palace' in Sawbridgeworth on the border of Hertfordshire and Essex. Media-savvy Victoria made a virtual tour of the mansion available online.

However, no WAG's life would be complete without scandal. Duly, on 4 April 2004, the *News of the World* reported that David Beckham had an affair with his personal assistant Rebecca Loos. At the time Beckham had left Manchester Union for Real Madrid and David was 'a lonely man in a foreign country,' the paper said. He was seen out on the town with team-mates Cristiano Ronaldo or Roberto Carlos, both of whom split with their own wives within a year of joining the club. Beckham dismissed this accusation as 'ludicrous'.

A close family friend of Rebecca's was sympathetic: 'He is a very sensitive guy and is so hurt because Victoria is ignoring him. The affair is a surprise to no one who knows him. He's been going weeks without sex, trying to stay faithful to her. But something had to give.'

While Ms Loos would not talk to the paper, the *News of the World* had managed to get a photograph of her with David in Madrid in September the previous year and reported that they had just kissed in public after playing a 'sexy game of truth or dare'.

Victoria Beckham, who was back in England pursuing her music career, got to hear of it. She phoned Rebecca to warn her off her man: 'It is not your job to go out clubbing with my husband so back off.'

She also gave Beckham 'an earbashing'. Afterwards, he phoned Rebecca and said, 'The s**t has hit the fan.'

Then Beckham broke off relations with the SFX Group, his former management company, where Rebecca worked.

Ms Loos was, of course, 'heartbroken.' Rebecca's brother John Charles told the *Daily Mail* that Loos feared being branded 'a marriage wrecker' and denied taking £300,000 from the *News of the World* and wept when the story appeared.

The London *Evening Standard* said that David was going to face a grilling from his wife when he flew out to meet the family for a skiing holiday in Switzerland. Pictures of the family cavorting in the snow were fetching £20,000 a time. The photographer Jason Fraser, who was said to have come across them by accident, was expected to make £250,000 out of them.

Bated, there was a spate of other ludicrous stories in the press. Beckham had been seen with thirty Swedish models in a nightclub in Basle, it was reported, and he had kissed one.

Pretty soon there was also a speculative blizzard of bimbos who claimed to have met up with a blonde football player for more than just friendship. A redhead called Helia claimed on Spanish TV that she had a liaison with an English footballer in a nightclub lavatory. Another woman thought she he had had a threesome with a blonde English footballer, even claiming she had photographs that could provide clues who it was. Twenty-three-year-old pneumatic Spanish model Nuria Bermudez—aka '*Muchas Tetas*'—also claimed to have slept with a blonde England player and was reputed to have bedded at least half the Real Madrid team.

'I started getting texts and he'd tell me things such as: "I am a real man and I'm going to show you what real men like me do",' she claimed about this macho footballer. 'He invited me to his hotel room two or three nights after the first texts and we had sex.'

She was touting her story around for £12,000, though there wasn't much of story in actual fact, apart from her ample epithet. She said that the texts had been erased when something went wrong with her SIM card. Meanwhile, Beckham's chauffeur Delfin Fernandez reckoned he could get £500,000 for his story about where he would drive Beckham while in Spain—though there were no bidders who agreed with him.

Loos herself choked back her tears and succumbed to the financial blandishments of the Sunday tabloids to talk more about her friendship. Her bowdlerised texts were published, but it wasn't clear what they meant to say. Meanwhile, the *Sun* did claim that Loos had been involved in nude situations with known lesbians and a former Wimbledon tennis champion thought he had met her in intimate circumstances in Madrid.

From far away, Malaysian-born Sarah Marbeck now came forward with her story, claiming to have bedded an England player after they met in Singapore and who might also have been blonde. She was ushered to his room at the Shangri-La Hotel by a bodyguard, she said.

According to Ms Marbeck, who modelled for Armani, Gucci and Calvin Klein, they were soon both naked and having 'perfect, really passionate' sex.

It was soon revealed, though, that her story, such as it was, was made of a tissue of made believe. The boss of the agency she worked for said that Marbeck boasted about the famous men she had slept with, but that she had not mentioned a football player, blonde or otherwise, to him. He was also puzzled about the texts that had been published as, he said, she had lost two mobile phones since she had been in Australia.

Meanwhile Beckingham Palace remained aloof from all the headlines swirling around its perimeter and it was business as usual, apart from successfully suing the

News of the World and an American magazine for stories about the state of their marriage, forcing the American publication to admit despite the US's relaxed defamation laws that its reportage had in fact been a misrepresentation.

Beckham spent £1 million on diamonds for Victoria's thirtieth birthday and revealed they were trying for another child. Beckham did, however, turn down an appearance on the *Simpsons* after the show made jokes about the recent media interest in the handsome, ripped footballer.

Once asked what she would do if he had an affair, Posh had replied: 'It's easy to think I would throw him out, burn his clothes, but I actually think it would kill me. I'd die of a broken heart.'

Soon after, Beckham bade *adios* to Spain and the couple headed for Los Angeles where, according to the *Sun*, ravening packs of *Playboy* centrefolds lay in wait. He was going to a Galaxy far, far away. There were even stories that text-friend Rebecca Loos was not certain whether she would remain in Spain, though by then interest in anything ludicrous had waned.

The Beckhams had two more children and lived happily ever after as in a fairy WAGtale.

16
Wags Aloud

Girls Aloud's Cheryl Tweedy's fairy-tale romance with Chelsea defender Ashley Cole hit a reef on a far rockier shore. She was working as a judge on *The X Factor* in Britain, before making her abortive debut on the American version of the show, when her marriage was hit by scandal headlines. Topless model Sonia Wild said she received nude photographs of the footballer sent to her mobile phone. Ashley said that he had not sent them. What had happened was, he had given the phone away, forgetting to delete the pictures first.

It had all started out so well. Before she met Ashley, Cheryl was coming off the back of criminal trial which saw her sentenced to 120 hours of community service after assaulting toilet attendant Sophie Amogbokpa in 2003. But, after a twenty-one-month relationship Ashley, things had turned around as Cheryl found herself being proposed to in a desert in Dubai. Afterwards, she said: 'I couldn't believe it when he popped the question but now I can't wait to be a footballer's wife.'

But the wedding had to wait until after the 2006 World Cup. She flew to Germany with the other WAGs. They married soon after on 15 July.

Cheryl said she had always wanted her wedding to be a small, quiet family gathering. Instead it was a star-studded WAG affair that shaded Sheryl and Gazza's tying the knot and took place at Wrotham Park, an eighteenth-century Palladian mansion set in 2,500 acres of countryside. A horse-drawn carriage with blacked-out windows carried her to the nearby church. The ceremony was attended by a gospel choir and angel harpists, while the reception overflowed with a constant stream of pink champagne. *OK!* Paid a whopping £500,000 for the exclusive rights and even the couple' pet chihuahua, Buster, got to wear a special wedding outfit.

Cheryl knew her business. By 2009, she had overtaken Victoria Beckham as Britain's top-earning WAG. The *News of the World* said: 'It's the end of Posh Spice's reign. Queen Victoria is on her way out. And there's a new princess ready to take her crown.'

The *Daily Telegraph*'s Bryony Gordon dubbed her a 'Princess Diana for the X Factor generation.'

It didn't rain but pour plaudits for her. A style icon, she adorned the covers of British *Vogue, Elle* and *Harper's Bazaar*, won several awards as the world's best-dressed woman and topped *FHM* magazine's 100

Sexiest Women in the World list in 2009 and 2010. Also, in 2010 she came second to Kylie Minogue as the most powerful celebrity in Britain and her wax work appeared in Madame Tussauds where it ruled for nine years.

But soon after her wedding there were rumours that Ashley was partying hard after away matches. Just eighteen months into their marriage twenty-two-year-old hairdresser Aimee Walton told the *Sun* that they had had a wild drinking night with Cole and his team mates. He had been out on a binge with his mates, downing vodka cocktails and chatting to women. The soccer-player was drunk and Aimee's friend offered to give him a lift to Cole's friend's place. He then vomited in the car. Aimee's friend was angry, but he retorted: 'She should be privileged Ashley Cole was sick in her car.' When they arrived at his friend's place, 'it wasn't long before he said he felt sick again,' she said. 'Then he just rolled over and vomited on the floor, all over the cream carpet. It was disgusting.', she said and not long after his friends piled into the room.

Cheryl immediately went to the *News of the World* and said that the Cole had told her about the bender and that she couldn't understand why Walton had gone to the papers to. 'All he could remember is his friends leaving him upstairs with this girl and him being so ill that he was sick and she was putting a bucket under his head, looking after him'. She saw some of the vomit on his clothes and gave Cole a yellow card when he returned, making him sleep on the sofa.

Two days later the *Sunday Mirror* carried more clubbing claims. Glamour model Brooke Healy said that Cole had partied with her at a Christmas party just five months after his wedding. She said that they met in the trendy club Funky Buddha in London's Mayfair when the Chelsea players were having their Christmas night out in 2006. Within minutes of walking to the swanky club, he had chatted to her. The party went on a nearby casino and, in order to avoid the paparazzi, they left separately with the group, and from there on to a friend's place. There they talked again and he was playful. 'He grabbed my head and neck,' she said. 'I was telling him not to pull my hair because I had extensions in. He was laughing and saying, 'I'm used to it with Cheryl'. Later, however, his mood had turned and he had been 'stand-offish' and 'a bit cold'. 'I felt a bit hurt,' she said, though he thoughtfully offered her £300 to get a cab home.

She declined but a few weeks later, she said, a friend of Ashley's approached her and got to sign a piece of paper saying that she would not go to the papers about the bender. The friend, she claimed, offered her £7,000. Brooke's name had been linked before to other soccer players who liked clubbing, but she told earlier told the press about her social life that 'I don't intentionally target football players—it's just the way it goes.'

About the footballers whom she would go on to date she confessed, 'People might call me a WAG but why date other men if I can date a football star? They're so fit—and they always satisfy you'.

Another woman turned up at the *Mirror* offices, saying that she had had a WAG relationship with Ashley Cole before he had started dating Cheryl. New Zealand-born actress Coralie Robinson also salaciously claimed she had been unimpressed by his prowess in the bedroom. But as her name has been linked to Robbie Williams, Russell Brand, Shane Warne and Ziggy from *Big Brother*, he was perhaps up against some stiff competition. According to the *Mirror*, she was given £10,000 and asked to sign the document in return for destroying all text messages, telephone messages and notes relating to her time with Cole.

One clause said: 'While I know A [Ashley Cole] as a friend, I have never at any time had a sexual relationship of any nature with him. Notwithstanding the non-sexual nature of my relationship with A I will keep all matters passing between A and myself and all information regarding A as a result of such relationship in the strictest confidence.' Nevertheless, Robinson decided it was her wont to tell her story to the tabloids.

But there other WAG worries to come. It was revealed that Cole had sent amusing texts to soccer-club secretary Vicki Gough. They occurred when Chelsea were playing away at Hull, only a month after

Cheryl had spoken to the *News of the World.*

At 1.12 pm on 27 October 2008 he sent a text saying: 'Mayb ill get another room what do u think x.' It was the beginning of a ping pong match of jokey messages. In all, she reckoned that she got over three hundred texts from Cole, some with shots of him standing in front of a mirror for a laugh. Later, he texted: 'I beg u to keep this between us x. Please delete all texts.' Following the events, Vicki left the club 'by mutual consent'.

Then news came that, on a US tour with the club, Cole had spent a party night in Seattle. He was celebrating their victory over the Seattle Sounders when he talked to twenty-eight-year-old Ann Corbitt as the team was celebrating at their hotel.

She in turn talked to the *News of the World* after he had sent her a picture of himself which didn't please her. 'He looked really skinny and was smoking a cigarette,' she said, perhaps used to health-conscious two hundred pound American Football players. 'I thought it was really gross. Just nasty.'

At the hotel, someone spilt beer on the floor, which splashed on her leg. In his euphoria about the game's success 'Ashley immediately grabbed it and licked the mess off,' she said. 'That really grossed me out.' After visiting a club, Ashley kicked two 'trashy-looking blondes' out of the team bus to make room for her.

The next day Ann was mortified by having joined

the team on its victory night and she texted Cole and asked him to not mention . Ashley called back, saying that no one had said that to him before. And, like a gentleman, he promised not to say a word.

But when a reporter got wind of the boozy night and visited Ann, she phoned Ashley. He begged her to call Steve Atkins, head of communications at Chelsea, who gave her advice on how to handle the press which she accepted, until she didn't.

Once again Cole was in the news because of Corbitt, and now glamour model Alexandra Taylor came forward to claim that he had WAGged her just before Ashley and Cheryl first started dating. Alexandra had been at the bar in Funky Buddha when Ashley went over to Alexandra to chat to her. Then he invited her back to party at his place with his friends. His friends ushered her passed the photographers to a waiting car. Back at his flat, Ashley wasted no time.

'He was really hands on and flirty when we got back there,' she said. 'We were both attracted to each other— it was really intense. After about fifteen minutes he said, 'I'm going upstairs to lie down,' and as he went, he gave me the eye to follow him.' Leaving the others downstairs she trotted off after him.

'When I got up there Ashley was already undressed and under the covers, just wearing his boxers,' she told the *Daily Mirror*. 'We were both really drunk, started kissing—and one thing led to another. He was so off his face with drink, he could barely do the deed. It lasted about fifteen minutes and was really lousy.'

'I tried to get some conversation out of him afterwards, but he just wanted to roll over and go to sleep. It was like he had got what he wanted and that was all he cared about.' Alexandra was a formidable conversationalist, or at least she was when she talked to the *Daily Mirror*.

The glamour model left the soccer star snoozing and got a cab home. Two days later, the story broke that Cheryl and Ashley were now an item. Although Ashley and Alexandra continued to see each other socially, he obviously did not give her a return match.

One of his friends called up to asked her to keep quiet about their entanglement, she said. She said nothing, fearing it would damage her modelling career. But she overcame that fear later.

'I wish I had gone public—or at least tried to let Cheryl know what her man was like,' she told the *Mirror* about their club night.

Amid the headlines, Cheryl announced she was leaving her husband and began divorce proceedings. She said that she would not take a penny from him, making a clean break. She was after all making more money than he was. However, she would continue to use his name.

Ashley barely missed a stride and looked for a new WAG. By October 2011, the newspapers were reporting that, soon after, he had pulled a pair of twins who had posed for *Playboy*. He got twenty-one-year-old Carla and Melissa Howe to parade outside their home to see which would get the chance to sleep with him. Melissa won and was whisked off to the Surrey home where Ashley had lived with Cheryl. Two days later, after a gig at the O2, he went off with one of Rihanna's dancers. Nevertheless, after four dates, Cole begged Melissa to move in with him, according to the *People*. She declined the offer, for the moment.

'I don't want him to think I'm one of those girls who just jumps into bed,' she said. 'And it's a bit too soon to be moving in, to be honest. Ashley is really good looking and has a good body. He seems like a really nice guy too. I think he is pretty besotted and things could get serious. But I'm only twenty-one and I'm making him wait.'

She should have seized the opportunity while WAGgery was on offer. In September 2010, the divorce was granted in under a minute, but soon the transfer window was closed. Cheryl was the real deal and a Queen WAG, while others were only one-day WAGs. By January 2011, the papers were reporting that Cheryl still had feelings for Ash. These feelings were, apparently, reciprocated. In July, the *Sun* reported that Ashley was planning to ask Cheryl to marry him again with a wedding ring carrying a diamond so big 'it is visible from space'. Hope sprang eternal.

It didn't happen. She went on to marry French restaurateur Jean-Bernard Fernandez-Versini. After they split, she had a relationship with One Direction singer Liam Payne and they had one child, baby Bear, together until they amicably separated in 2018. Though no longer a WAG, she had become what Sheryl Kyle had striven for at the end of her marriage to Gazza—a media star in her own right who drew paparazzi like bees to honey.

Cole had two children with Italian model Sharon Canu. In 2006, he sued the *News of the World* and the *Sun* newspapers for libel after they printed allegations that he was once involved in an orgy. Both papers retracted the allegations as being untrue.

17
Given the Wagaround

David Beckham's teammate at Manchester, Ryan Giggs got himself into hot water over WAGs. In May 2011, the foreign media reported that Welsh international Giggs was 'CTB', in the anonymised action CTB v News Group Newspapers, a gagging order the footballer had taken out over alleged extra-marital affair with model Imogen Thomas, a former Miss Wales and *Big Brother* star. Giggs then ill-advisedly took legal action against the social networking site Twitter after he was named as one of those who had secured so-called 'super-injunctions'. This only increased interest in the story and the press starting circling. Using parliamentary privilege Lib-Dem MP John Hemmings named Ryan Giggs as the person who had taken out the super-injunction.

Then his sister-in-law Natasha Giggs dropped a bombshell. Natasha was married to Ryan's brother Rhodri, who played for Torquay and Salford. She had always been frank. On the website Friends Reunited, she boasted of 'a decent social life, usually out in town lookin too drunk to be a mother of 2!!!!' She also listed her hobbies as 'shopping, socialising, drinking'.

On 5 June 2011, the *News of the World* printed a full confession that twenty-eight-year-old Natasha had given via a friend. 'Anything he said, I did. If he wanted me to drop everything to meet him, I would. I just couldn't say no.' She was besotted with her brother in law 'There were constant calls, constant texts', she confessed, 'But Ryan was never romantic with me.'

Her absorption with Giggs was no small matter. Ryan Giggs was a Unicef ambassador and he had been awarded an honorary degree by the University of Salford for his football and charity work, and an OBE. His image had helped him become equal twentieth in the *Sunday Times Sport Rich List* with an estimated fortune of £34 million—much of it from endorsement and sponsorship. In an interview he said: 'My family is the most important thing to me.'

After dating TV presenter Dani Behr, Giggs had briefly been engaged to ex-*Hollyoaks* actress Davinia Taylor until they fell out following an incident at a Manchester club. He later WAGged Emma Gardner, sister of his former United youth teammate Dave Gardner, but the relationship didn't last. Four years later he went out with Stacey Cooke who already had WAG credentials. She was Gardner's ex-fiancée. Ryan and Stacey married in 2007.

In 2011 rumours circulated that Imogen Thomas had been sleeping with a footballer. Natasha texted Giggs to ask if he was the player involved. He replied a very stern denial: 'No way. It's not me.'

The rumours persisted, but Giggs dismissed them as a joke. Then posts on a blog remarked on the same player having a relationship with Natasha. Natasha got emails from people she had not spoken to for ages asking: 'Is it true'? Then her sister's boyfriend got a call from a girl he knew asking: 'What's the gossip about Natasha?'

'I emailed the girl back myself and said, "What do you want to know?"' Natasha said. But she went on step further. Natasha also spoke to a newspaper how she had first met Ryan in a Manchester nightclub in March 2003. She was twenty and had recently split from the father of her first child.

'Ryan was with another footballer at the Sugar Lounge. He came over to me and started buying drinks,' Natasha said. 'He complimented me on my eyes and teeth, and, at the end of the evening, he took my number and asked me to meet him the following night. I admit I was star-struck.'

They met the next night at The Living Room bar in Manchester where she also met his brother Rhodri. She and Ryan had got separated at one point. 'I must have looked upset because Rhodri told me to cheer up and I snapped, 'Where's your brother?' Those were my first words to Rhodri,' she said.

She and Ryan moved on to the nearby Circle night-club, then on for a Chinese meal. 'When I got home and told my mum she said she'd read that Ryan had a girlfriend who was pregnant. But to be honest, even that didn't throw me,' Natasha said.

She did not hear from Giggs for two weeks, then he got back in touch. 'We started going out a lot, always in a group of friends, and always to those same places', she said, 'But we never once spoke about Stacey or the baby he was expecting.'

In May she started dating Rhodri. The next time she met Ryan was at a New Year's party at his mother's house. Natasha said. 'It was a nerve-racking situation for me. Ryan was polite all evening but later contacted me and said, "I can't believe you're seeing our kid!" After that, he didn't see me for a year.'

In July 2005, Natasha accepted Rhodri's proposal of marriage. He wanted Ryan to be best man, but it was not to be. Natasha and Ryan did not meet again until his mother's fiftieth birthday party.

In 2009 Rhodri spotted them texting at a party. 'Rhodri went absolutely mad, grabbed my mobile, saw a few messages then smashed the phone on the floor,' Natasha confessed. 'I managed to grab my SIM', she added, 'But in any case, I always saved Ryan's number in my phone under UKW which stands for You Know Who.'

Apparently consumed with guilt, Natasha vowed to put a stop to her infatuation in March 2011. 'I told Ryan, "I think I need to give you up for Lent. You're becoming a bit of an addiction,"' she said.

'I never had any intention of hurting Rhodri, but I know that's what I have done,' she said. 'He will feel really humiliated and betrayed. I don't think he'll ever speak to me again. I don't think he'll ever forgive me.'

After Natasha had told all to the newspapers, she could not face Rhodri. She wrote him a note before fleeing their £189,000 home in Bolton and escaped into hiding. In the note, she said simply: 'You'll be reading something about me tomorrow'—then fled to Spain.

'Rhodri is devastated—he just can't get his head round it,' said a family friend. 'Natasha just wrote him a letter and disappeared, she didn't even tell him face to face. Rhodri says she's ruined his life—everything has changed for him now for the worst.'

Rhodri got a phone call from Ryan, who stated there was never an affair. 'Ryan called him but he's still denying everything at the minute,' the family friend said.

A source told the *Irish Sun*: 'Ryan and Rhodri have finally spoken on the telephone. Let's just say it was a frank exchange of views. Ryan tried to tell Rhodri that the whole thing was rubbish and not true. Rhodri went on, 'It doesn't make any sense'.

'Eventually Stacey grabbed the phone off Ryan and

started shouting, "Look, Rhodri, if it's not true, it's just not true. We don't believe Natasha". She then hung up.'

Ryan flew out to Majorca with Stacey to get away from all the rumours. Stacey suspected foul play on behalf of Natasha. 'He has gone on to become one of the best players in the country and a pin-up, and she knows the attention he attracts from all types of women,' said Stacey's friend. 'She can deal with that, but I don't think she quite expected that attention to come from someone so close. Make no bones about it, Stacey believes Natasha has been trying for years to steal her husband. She's suspected it for some time and these events prove it. But she has not succeeded. Ryan has stayed with Stacey and is a wonderful father to their children.'

'When Natasha realised she couldn't have Ryan, she settled for poor Rhodri instead,' the friend said. 'She made do with the next best thing and always knew the real Giggs would still be in her life, hoping one day he'd be hers. We all just feel for Stacey. She has done nothing wrong and yet has been dragged into the spotlight through no fault of her own by one disgusting allegation after another.'

Stacey was ill-equipped for the WAG scrutiny of the tabloids. 'Stacey is not the typical WAG,' said the friend. 'She has never wanted to be in the limelight. She values her privacy and just wants a quiet life. She will be devastated by all this. But she definitely won't let Natasha win.'

Then topless pictures of Natasha taken by an old boyfriend surfaced: one featured a close-up of her bottom in a sexy pink thong. The vendor also claimed to have more explicit pictures of Natasha. He said she had posed for the pictures around the time she first met Giggs.

A friend told the *Daily Star*: 'She is mortified and angry that anyone would try to cash in on her misery.' However, she was not above cashing in on it herself, giving another exclusive interview to the *News of the World.*

'Ryan just thinks he's untouchable,' she told the newspaper. 'We'd go out with friends to clubs and pubs.' Things had first begun to unravel in November 2005, when Natasha and her mates met Ryan and his mates in Manchester as he was out celebrating his birthday. They moved on to the Panacea nightclub, but Natasha was shocked when a friend told her Stacey was also there.

'At that point I thought this was really suspect, so my friend and I went somewhere else,' said Natasha. 'Then I remember looking at my phone and I had fifteen missed calls. Ryan was just like, 'Where are you?' He was really annoyed and said Stacey was asking, "Why has she left?"' 'We'd flirt with each other and send each other pictures,' she said about her obsession with Ryan.

But she bumped into him at a garage in Worsley. 'As

Ryan pulled up next to me, I couldn't even speak,' said Natasha. 'He was like, 'Are you OK? You've not texted me.' I told him I was fine, and I drove off. Then he rang me saying, 'Is everything OK?' and I said, 'Not really.' I said, 'When you've finished with your meeting give me a ring. I need to speak to you.' And he said, 'Well I can talk now.' Obviously he knew something was going on. It was awful. I was crying.'

She then admitted to the paper that she had slept with Rhodri's best friend Will Mellor, but that had been eleven years earlier, before he had met Rhodri. Then there was Dwight Yorke. Again, that was before she knew Rhodri.

'And then there were the times when Rhodri and I were on a break. That was when I was briefly with Danny Simpson. Then again, I had a short fling with Phil Bardsley before he had a girlfriend.

She had been a WAG to other footballers. 'It's not that I go out hunting down footballers, they are just people I know,' she said.

A friend of Giggs's said the footballer had told him that he had had a fling with Natasha, but it was short-lived and well before either of them were married.

'Me and Natasha getting together is old news,' he said. 'It happened years ago and Rhodri has always known. It wasn't great between us all when it came out but we got over it and I thought we'd all put it behind us.' He was relieved that he had managed to convince

Stacey that Natasha was overegging her side of the story.

'That's all he's bothered about,' the friend said. 'It's what Stacey thinks that's important to him—and at the moment she believes Natasha is making a lot of it up.'

About Natasha, Rhodri was reported as saying: 'The funny thing is I still love you so much... you've been so stupid.' One newspaper said that Rhodri had gone to the Circle club until 4am to get over Natasha twenty-four hours after she split with him and he was taking selfies with a hen party. He was 'I wouldn't say he looked sad,' said thirty-five-year-old Michelle Bates. 'He was just like a regular guy. He was just really friendly, and he gave all of us a kiss goodbye.' Even so, they were to divorce in 2013, thought they would remain good friends.

Rhodri himself became a target for stories. Wannabe WAG Danielle Heally also came forward to say how she had once met Rhodri in a pub in Worsley, where the Giggs brothers had grown up.

'I was out with friends and Rhodri was sitting on the next table with Will Mellor and another lad,' she said. 'We started chatting when they called last orders and they asked where the party was going to be. We went back to someone's house and started doing karaoke. Rhodri was up there singing away.

'I noticed he had rings on both hands. He was banging his right hand on a table and one mate asked,

'Is that your wedding ring?'

'Rhodri held up his left hand and said, 'No, that's my wedding ring.' Then he pointed to his right hand and said, 'That's my divorce ring.' I just thought it was a throwaway comment.'

Danielle said Rhodri and she bumped into each other in a hallway later. 'We were laughing and joking, and we'd had a fair bit to drink', she added. 'Then these two random women turned up. I think Rhodri's friends had called them.' Everyone left at about 3.30am and Danielle said about the end of the meeting. 'I didn't think much about it after that as I knew he was married', she added, 'but I had his number and decided to text him just to make sure he was all right.'

Rhodri replied: 'I'm fine thanks. Just didn't want you emailing me on the off-chance, Natasha checks my emails. Hope you're well and maybe see you soon. I knew he was trying to watch his back, so I decided to leave it alone.'

18
Wags, Not Slags

In a philosophical editorial about footballers, the *Sun* noted that 'The problem isn't 'sluts'… it's WAGs.' The Giggs' story had 'once again shone a torchlight into the murky corners of Britain's nightclubs and bars, where young women display questionable tactics in their bid to secure their rich and famous 'prize'. Thoughtfully musing further, the paper noted 'Their poster girls are women like Ryan Giggs' wife Stacey or Toni Terry— last seen wearing a thong bikini.'

Natasha had been hiding out in Spain. When she returned to Manchester after ten days, she was clearly pregnant. She announced her return on Facebook, saying: 'Natasha Giggs is back!! If you don't like it, you know where the 'unfriend' button is.' She added: 'Once a good girl's gone bad, she's gone forever.'

When it came to Danielle Healy, she said: 'Dunno whether to slap her or shake her hand!!!!' Earlier she had penned: 'No need for revenge; just sit back and wait. Eventually the one that hurt you will screw up and if you're lucky you'll get to watch!'

The post was accompanied by a selfie showing off her topped-up suntan, of course. 'I've had 10 days in Spain on top of my profile pic,' she crowed. She also said that she was planning a girls' night out to find a new man.

A friend told the *Daily Star*: 'As far as Natasha is concerned, her new life starts here. She's confessed her sins, cleaned out her closet and is ready to start over. If Ryan and Rhodri were hoping she'd quietly disappear, they'd better get real. She's pissed off with both of them and hinted there are more revelations to come.'

According to the *Sunday Mirror*, her hunt for a new man had already started with a holiday fling with twenty-four-year-old Gary Barlow impersonator Ashley Crowe, singer with the tribute band Fake That. They met at the Jimmy Hill's bar in the resort of Cala'n Forcat where he was performing. Playing on her status as an ex-WAG, she introduced herself to his in the crowded bar, saying: 'Hi, I'm Natasha Giggs.'

She invited him back to her hotel room for a drink. 'Let's just say it was a lot of fun,' Ashley told a friend. But Natasha denied they had sex.

Meanwhile Ryan Giggs started legal action against the *News of the World* for hacking his phone. Rhodri started legal action of his own by dropping divorce papers through Natasha's letterbox on the day of their first wedding anniversary.

In an effort to expedite matters the divorce papers provided by Rhodri's solicitors included a confession for Natasha which said simply she admitted committing adultery with 'a man'.

Imogen Thomas still sought to cash in on her status as a temporary WAG. She was in discussion about making a new realty TV dating show *Imogen Finds A Husband*. She was also seen sporting a temporary tattoo saying: 'Liars and cheats will never have my heart.'

Stacey, wearing a white designer beach dress over a blue halter-neck bikini but no wedding ring, was nursing her broken heart with a dose of retail therapy in Palma, while Giggs tagged along behind in black swimming shorts. They were staying in a £22,000-a-week, seven-bed villa with its own concierge, nanny and chef.

Natasha told the *Daily Star*, 'I know that at the back of her mind she'll be constantly wondering what he's up to. For the money and a WAG's lifestyle, is the humiliation and stress worth it? I don't think so'. She added mournfully, 'I can start again and find the right man for me with no secrets. I suggest Stacey should do the same.'

She added: 'I was his lapdog who would come running whenever he wanted.... I am just so glad Ryan is out of my life—and next time I see him I won't be as shy in saying so.'

Natasha also announced that she wanted to give up

the WAG status that had propelled her into the public eye. Posing for a sexy photo shoot, she said: 'I no longer want to be a Giggs. As soon as my divorce is through, I am changing back to my maiden name Lever.'

She said she was going to find somewhere new to live where she could have a normal life with her sons. Nevertheless, she was seen having a shouting match with Rhodri in the street.

Stacey seemed to think Natasha's advice. The *Daily Star* reported that she and Ryan were trying for another child—and wanted Rhodri to be godfather. She was also giving the £5-million home an expensive makeover so the couple could start afresh. A carpenter has been commission to build a bespoke four-poster bed which she hoped was completed by the time they returned from holiday.

However, after a dressing down by Alex Ferguson, Giggs was off on a pre-season tour of the US where he was spotted dancing on a table with a scantily clad belly dancer at the Lavo club in New York. When he returned to Manchester, he had to accompany Stacey for more retail therapy.

Two months later, when they were out shopping again, Stacey and Ryan bumped into Natasha. Within seconds they were having a blazing row. One witness told the *Daily Star* that Giggs accused her of selling her story of their affair for a six-figure sum to fund her recent boob job which cost her £4,250.

'Giggs was going nuts,' 'the witness said. 'He lost the plot completely. At one point he shouted at her: "Pay for your boobs did it?"'

Their slanging match even brought traffic to a standstill. It went on for ten minutes and staff from a restaurant came out to check no-one was hurt.

Later Natasha posted: 'That awkward moment when you bump into the one person you never thought you'd see again.'

A follower replied: 'I hate them moments… jesus it wasnt RG was it??'

Natasha responded: 'Ha the one n only!!! Had a blazin row in the street he is such a tit!!!!!!!! xx It was mental!!!!'

A bawl by bawl report continued on Twitter.

Asked if she was still with Rhodri, she replied: 'We are friends yes.' She was then blitzed by United fans.

'Im the easy target, im sure if he was on twitter he'd get the same,' she replied.

To a female United supporter who slammed her, Natasha replied: 'Hi darlin, thanks for the err "comments", jus had a look at your bio. . Ryan is your idol?' She added: 'Listen, im not defending myself for what i did?? I never have!! I was wrong, i held my hands up' and concluded, 'Bore off!!! Im a 29 year old woman, i fight my own battles… REGARDLESS!!!'

Then backstage at a music festival in Leeds, Natasha

posed with Oasis frontman Liam Gallagher who was City fan known to hate United. He was chuffed and kept saying: 'This is mint.'

Natasha then turned to the *Sunday Mirror*. She said the incident had occurred on her twenty-ninth birthday when she had gone to pick her sister up in Worsley. Ryan and Stacey were just coming out of a Chinese restaurant.

'I slowly looked round and he was there on the pavement, eyes bulging, staring right at me,' Natasha said. 'I could see he was ranting, raving and swearing.'

He caught up with her when her car was stopped in rush-hour traffic. With his face pressed up against the window, he ordered her to wind it down. He then launched into a tirade of abuse as passers-by looked on astonished when Stacey joined him.

'I always knew I'd bump into him at some point,' Natasha said. 'But there couldn't have been a worse situation—in the street, with Stacey, on my birthday.'

She said that, when Ryan had denied everything, she found herself in the extraordinary position of having to prove to her husband that she was sleeping with his brother.

Meanwhile she was still trying to patch things up with Rhodri.

'I love Rhodri and I will always love him,' she said. 'And I am confident he will always love me. As far as us being together… I am not ruling it out.'

They had days out with the kids and he often had Sunday lunch with her parents. He even planned to be with Natasha and the boys on Christmas Day.

'We'll go to the park with the boys, feed the ducks, go to the pub for something to eat,' she said. 'People see us looking like we are a couple and I think that is hard for him. When he comes round, he uses the back door even though he has a key. I have so much admiration for Rhodri.'

Stacey meanwhile broke the 'no wives' rule Manchester United players Christmas party, turning up in glamorous, low-cut black trouser suit. Imogen Thomas was seen wearing an almost identical trouser suit clubbing in Brentford, Essex.

But Natasha was not to be kept out of the limelight. She told the *Sun*: 'At the beginning it was thrilling'. Yet she said, 'there was nothing romantic about it.'

She now slept alone in the bed she used to share with Rhodri and was eager to make up with him. 'I learned two crucial things this year—the most important being that I love my husband more than I ever realised. I still can't believe what a fool I was.'

'I hope time can heal the pain I've caused. This has been the worst year of my life and I know I only have myself to blame for the way things turned out,' she said. '

Natasha then went on to appear on *Celebrity Big Brother*, where it was ex-WAG against WAG, Page 3 girl

Nicola McLean, wife of Kettering Town defender Tom Williams. Soon it was war again.

'If she goes on the show, she is just making money from ruining people's lives,' said Nicola. 'I know everyone has a past but, to me, it's the lowest of the low.'

Natasha responded by calling Nicola a 'fake Barbie doll' and a 'busy arse with no life of her own'. Nicola also called Imogen a slag. The former Miss Wales had claimed that Nicola's husband Tom had 'wandering eyes'.

'My husband is faithful—fact,' Nicola hissed back.

Natasha's sisters Haley and Kerrie Lever rallied to her defence.

'Natasha is the best sister anyone could ask for and she made a mistake,' they said. 'We're all very loyal in our family and we stick together. We don't agree with what she's done but she's admitted it, taken the flak and apologised. It's not been easy for her.' Haley went to hospital with Natasha when she had an abortion. She also accompanied Natasha on her flight to Spain while Kerrie remained in Manchester to deliver the letter confessing all to Rhodri.

The sisters said they were proud of how Natasha has faced her demons by admitting everything to Rhodri and facing the public in the Big Brother house.

After a 'year of hell' mini-WAG Imogen found happiness with twenty-five-year-old Australian city trader Adam Horsley, though she said she would never marry.

She also told the *Sun* that she hated being described as a WAG.

'That label annoyed me. I wasn't that person and I've only been out with two or three footballers,' she said. 'If I was that person, I'd be marrying one now—but I'm with a normal person.'

She warned other women to beware of footballers, saying: 'You're not going to be treated nice by them. Most footballers think they're invincible and that they can get away with murder. It's the world they live in....'

'They've got a lot of money and the lifestyle that goes with it and some girls want that. It seems quite lucrative when you look at it. A lot of girls think, 'I could have a bit of that."

Imogen said that her own time in the headlines had driven her to antidepressants and drink.

'But with the drinking comes the tears,' she said. 'I didn't want to go out, I wasn't in the mood, and I was scared someone would glass me.'

She suffered abuse and death threats, even moving house for her own safety. At one point she even considered suicide but pulled through with the help of her family.

After having two children with Adam Horsley, the couple split. Imogen launched her own brand of swimwear which she modelled herself. Although she said she had hated being a WAG, the *Daily Mirror* reported that like to move on footballer Jamie

Redknapp, though he was said to having been growing closer to his ex, Louise, singer with the girl group Eternal.

'I'm a bit bored of being single now, my ideal is Jamie,' she told *New!* magazine. 'I'm going to slide into his DMs and say "Hi." I actually don't want to be a WAG, but Jamie seems really kind and he's gorgeous.'

While Natasha and Rhodri divorced, Stacey and Ryan were seen sunbathing together in the South of France two years later. However, in 2016, Stacey told Ryan to pack his bags after she was told that he had been seen flirting with waitresses at George's, a Manchester restaurant he owned. For a time though they continued living in the same house. By then Natasha had a third child with her new partner Mark Smith.

'Stacey is devastated, but she can't see any way back,' the friend said about the intended divorce. Then it was revealed that Giggs sent flowers to thirty-two-year-old PR girl Kate Greville who was helping him promote Hotel Football which overlooked Old Trafford. Her picture appeared on the front page of the *Sun*. She had recently ended her eighteen-month marriage to a United fan, but she left to work in Abu Dhabi. Katie Price also claimed that Giggs flirted with her. She told *Loose Women* that he was 'charming, but intense'.

As a result of the media reports, the Giggs' marital home was then spray-painted with graffiti. This upset their twelve-year-old daughter Liberty Beau. Her grand-mother said: 'Stacey does not deserve this.'

Stacey was later seen out at Club Liv in Manchester with fellow WAG Emma Neville, wife of Ryan's team-mate Gary. She was wearing a gold sequinned jacket over a white vest top, but no wedding ring, and seemed to be holding back the tears as she clung on to Emma's hand.

More pain was to come when he was seen flirting with actress Stephanie Davis, former star of *Hollyoakes* and *Celebrity Big Brother*.

'He told her she had 'a great figure' and laughed at all her jokes,' the *Sun* reported. They were planning a meal out together. Stacey's response was to have the word 'free' tattooed on her neck. Nevertheless, Ryan was still seen wearing his wedding ring.

That summer he took Stacey and the kids on holiday at the £500-a-night Conrad Hotel in Quinta do Lago in the Algarve. He was seen breakfasting alone and she would wine and dine with friends.

His attempts to save his marriage finally ended in January 2017 when he finally caved in to his wife's demand for a divorce. They were divorced on the grounds of unreasonable behaviour that summer. The hearings were held in private and a legal order prevent-ed publication of the financial settlement. Stacey had been asking for half his £40-million fortune. He argued he had made a 'special contribution' to the creation of wealth during the marriage.

Then Kate Greville re-appeared as Head of PR and Communications at GG Hospitality, a company Giggs owns with his former Man-U teammate Gary Neville. They broke up after she started having secret Botox treatments, splashed out on designer clothes and was receiving expensive gifts, including a £600 Mulberry handbag. Giggs was spotted giving her a lift to work in his £100,000 Range Rover, clutching a £1,000 Louis Vuitton overnight bag.

Paul Gascoigne could not help putting his oar in, teasing Ryan Giggs and Wayne Rooney, who the *Sunday Mirror* reported had slept with a forty-eight-year-old grandmother.

'I'd have fitted in,' said Gazza.

Eight months after his divorce, Giggs went on holiday with Kate in Ravello on Italy's Amalfi coast. An onlooker said: 'Kate looks every inch a footballer's WAG and he looked pleased as punch to have such a trophy on his arm.'

She looked the part and wore a summer dress and a chic leather jacket, while he blended into the crowds in chinos and a polo shirt. The couple were seen sunbathing by the hotel's pool, with Kate looking toned in a red bikini. The *Sun* said: 'Surely he must score.' She also accompanied him to Moscow when he went to Russian to cover England's World Cup clash with Belgium.

At the age of forty, Stacey found love again with

thirty-year-old Max George from the boy band The Wanted. She was a massive fan. He was a regular guest at the Giggs's mansion which she took over after the divorce. They met in the John Gilbert pub in Worsley, Manchester—where Ryan and Natasha used to meet—and hit it off straight away. He had kept a low profile after leaving the band and splitting from Coronation Street star Michelle Keegan.

'Stacey deserves all the happiness she can get,' a friend said. 'And Max is quite a catch. She's been grinning like the Cheshire Cat.'

She splashed out on a £1,000-a-night penthouse suite in Ibiza for her first holiday with her new love. While Max was not short of a bob or two, she insisted on paying. He was a Manchester City fan.

He confirmed in the press that she was his girlfriend and they had matching tattoos. She put her home on the market and she and Max were house hunting with budget of £1.5-million. After appearing on *Strictly Come Dancing* in 2020, he said he was ready to have a baby with her.

Meanwhile in November 2020, Ryan Giggs was arrested for assaulting Kate and another woman thought to have been a relative of hers. The police were called and a spokesperson said: 'A woman in her thirties sustained minor injuries but did not require any treatment. A forty-six-year-old man was arrested on suspicion of section 47 assault and section 39 common assault.'

After being held overnight, he was released on bail pending enquiries and was whisked away in a black Mercedes. Banned from contacting Kate under his bail conditions, he sought refuge in one of the hotels he owned while Kate moved out, taking her puppy. Giggs was then charged with three offences in April 2021 at Manchester Magistrates with headbutting his partner while 'in drink' and subjecting her to 'degrading treatment', according to prosecutor Andrea Griffiths. He denied all charges and, pending trial he was granted bail conditional on not approaching them.

A source told the *Sun* newspaper about Kate, 'She was already struggling to trust him and then she found flirty messages he'd sent to other girls. She knows who they are. One works in London as a PR to a high-profile footballer, the other is a model based in Cheshire. They're both younger than Giggs and very glamorous.'

Giggs was accused of getting close to thirty-three-year-old former air hostess Zara Charles after 'flirty' phone messages were found. They had known each other for several years.

The *Sun*'s source said: 'She kept quiet about it until Sunday. In recent months she has found messages. There are flirty ones between him and a sports PR executive. Zara also featured in them, which aroused Kate's suspicions.'

19
The 2006 Wag Cup

2006 was the foundation year of Team WAG. French lingerie model and actress Vanessa Perroncel was dubbed a WAG when she was spotted alongside the glamorous other halves of the England football players during the 2006 World Cup where WAGgery truly grew up and blossomed into a full-fledged phenomenon. The top-flight included Victoria Beckham, Cheryl Tweedy (later Mrs Cole), Wayne Rooney's fiancée Coleen McLoughlin, Theo Walcott's sweetheart Melanie Slade, Michael Carrick's girlfriend Lisa Roughead, Steven Gerrard's missus Alex Curran and John Terry's fiancée Toni Poole.

Vanessa was the girlfriend of Chelsea and England player Wayne Bridge and went on to have his baby. Flying into Germany, she was seen wearing £180 Rock & Republic jeans designed by Posh Spice. Also in tow were Frank Lampard's fiancée Elen Rivas, Joe Cole's girlfriend Carly Zucker, Stewart Downing's partner Michaela Henderson-Thynne and Peter Crouch's lover, model Abigail Clancy.

Based in Baden-Baden they started with a boozy night out. At the Wintergarten restaurant, Coleen McLoughlin, Elen Rivas, Alex Curran, Carly Zucker and Abigail Clancy belted out a cover version of Queen's 'We Are The Champions'. Though they had wilted in the sunshine while their men played Paraguay, Coleen McLoughlin showed no signs of fatigue. After refreshing herself with pints of lager at the match, she finished off with vodka Red Bull in Maxi's nightclub where Elen Rivas danced on the table and entertained reporters singing along to 'I Will Survive'. Between them, they spent £400 on booze. The WAGs slept in that Sunday.

The next day, the WAG posse clocked up £57,000 on their credit cards in a one-hour lightning shopping blitz. That's nearly £1,000 a minute. They started at the Albert sunglasses shop where they bought several pairs of designer shades. Four of the WAGs each invested in Fred Lunettes and Gucci sunglasses that cost £500 a pair.

In ten minutes, Coleen McLoughlin snapped up two pairs of Gucci and Dior shoes and two Dolce and Gabbana blouses for around £900. The twenty-year-old was at the Monica Scholz designer shop. She said: 'I just wanted to come out for a walk, and I have bought some bits and pieces.'

Others picked up Gucci, D Squared, Manolo

Blahnik, Prada and Dolce Gabbana shoes and tops. After spending £3,000 on outfits they legged it to the Gero Mure fashion store, then Bijou Brigitte, picking up bracelets, earrings and rings along the way.

They bought Prada shoes at Andiamo at £1,200 a pair and stopped at Nanou to buy £1,000 dresses by Diane von Furstenberg and Chloe handbags at £6,000. The owner of Nanou Ilona Dressel-Witte said: 'They come every day, apart from Posh who we've not seen. They all want clothes. They love Blumarine, Chloe, Marni. They all have very good taste.'

And they were the perfect customers. 'They're so polite and they spend a lot of money,' Ilona said.

Twenty-nine-year-old Elen Rivas, who wore a see-through blouse, chino shorts and high heels, said: 'We are here to support the boys, but shopping is nice too.'

'It is very exciting, and the shops are great. We expect to be back here,' said twenty-year-old Michaela Henderson-Thynne, who wore denim shorts and slouchy boots.

Fitness instructor Carly Zucker wore a pair of candy-pink jeans and a shrunken top, while pilates teacher Lisa Roughead sported a turquoise top and white shorts, topped off with a studded belt and frumpy flatties. Both were twenty-four and were seen chatting during the shopping trip. The *Daily Mirror* speculated they were discussing Nancy Dell'Olio's outfit. She had arrived in Baden-Baden wearing a black vest top and an England bandana-style scarf, while twenty-five-year-old Vanessa Perroncel was relatively demure in a crumpled-look white dress.

Shop owner Monica Scholz said: 'We have had President Clinton here and Bono but I don't think they made as big a stir as these girls.'

Her husband Peter added: 'The England wives were lovely. The ladies love the labels we have here.'

Twenty-four-year-old Alex Curran bought a new mobile phone then went to McDonald's with the couple's kids—two-year-old Lilly and newborn daughter Lexie.

Victoria Beckham was notably absent from the shopping trip. She took Romeo, Brooklyn and Cruz to see Becks before going to their hotel.

'Perhaps old hand Posh didn't want to steal the limelight off the bright young things coming through the England shopping squad,' said the *Mirror*. The *Daily Telegraph* noted that the WAGs were fuelled by Red Bull and asked: 'When did shopping become a team sport?' And: 'Haven't they got enough Prada T-shirts already?'

'Shopping is a really good ice-breaker among women, because everyone can have an opinion,' said Jenny Summerfield, a psychologist and life coach. 'There's social affirmation and a social connection. If the England players' wives and girlfriends are looking for common ground, it's a good way to establish that. The junior members will want to impress the wives of more famous footballers in the team, so the pressure is on these women to get along with the rest of the group, whether that's through drinking or shopping.'

Retail outlets in Baden-Baden had bought in £200,000 of extra Gucci and Hermès stock to cater for England's WAGs. Germany's biggest paper *Bild* said: 'They spend more lolly in ten minutes than most of us spend on half our wardrobe in a lifetime. While the bread winners train for the next game the ladies improve their shopping condition. It has become Shopping-Shopping in Baden-Baden.'

Another boutique owner said: 'It is almost as if they want to shop the place dry of designer clothes. More money is being made in our fashion shops than anywhere else during the World Cup in Germany.'

But the *Daily Telegraph* remained unimpressed. It remarked that 'our finest footballers' wives looked more like a Top Shop staff outing than a gathering of sporting ambassadresses on a high-spending spree' and that Victoria Beckham 'must have been weeping into her tattered copy of Style Commandments as she surveyed the sartorial wreckage'.

Posh had flown in on a private jet, costing £21,000, after her scheduled flight was grounded in Madrid. She had brought sixty pairs of sunglasses with her—two a day even if England made it to the final. Brooklyn carried a £500 Yves Saint Laurent shoulder bag. This was outshone by Coleen McLoughlin's £800 Balenciaga bag and the £2,000 Fendi bag she was seen with at Manchester airport. Others flew in by Ryanair from Stansted.

Afterward they had shopped until they dropped, the WAGs relaxed beside the pool at the exclusive £1,000-a-night Brenner's Park hotel. One onlooker said: 'In their orange and yellow bikinis you could hardly miss them. They all looked like they had walked off the set of Baywatch. It is pretty clear that they have been working out for this moment.'

Swimming against the tide, Carly Zucker wore a black and white number, while Coleen McLoughlin's Liz Hurley beachwear cost £120.

Although it was sunny, the hotel had taken the precaution of importing large quantities of a fake tan called Fake Bake from England to make sure no WAG looked pasty.

'It's something very special in England. We don't have it in Germany,' a spokesman for the hotel said. On top of that Alex Curran and Coleen McLoughlin had bought two tan therapists with them at a cost of £15,000.

That evening the WAGs were out drinking again. The younger ones stayed out until 2am, but last to bed was Nancy Dell'Olio. The rest of the week was given up to drinking and sunbathing with Posh alienating the other by refusing to join in the singsong after England's victory over Trinidad and Tobago and upstaging them with her revealing outfits. But Coleen was not to be outdone. She was seen leaving the hotel in a £2,300 outfit which included Gucci sunglasses, Robert Cavalli shorts, a Fendi B handbag, costing almost £1,500 by itself, and Christian Louboutin heels.

Meanwhile, a columnist on *Bild* apologised for calling David Beckham's twenty-six-year-old sister Joanne a typical overweight English girl only interested in getting blind drunk in Ibiza. But then, she wasn't a WAG.

By the 2006 World Cup, WAG had become an established concept. The *Independent* even published: 'The Essential Guide to WAGs World Cup.'

It gave a quick rundown of the opposition England's WAGs faced. Pick of the bunch in Group A was Simone Lambe, the twenty-seven-year-old girl-friend of the Chelsea-bound German star Michael Ballack who wore a busty Bavarian blouse offset by a rib-crunching girdle.

In Group B there was Teressa Edwards, wife of Trinidad and Tobago's midfielder Carlos Edwards, who has aspirations to a pop career. Sweden presented a serious challenge in the shape of the country's most famous WAG Helena Segur and the catwalk model Anine Bing. But Paraguay's blonde bombshell, Giselle Santa Cruz, who was married to the striker, Roque Santa Cruz, was discounted as she had too much class.

In Group C, model and actress Sylvie Francoise van

der Vaart-Meis, wife of the Dutch star Rafael van der Vaart, had a fine bone structure 'offset by a tan so deep and luminous she is forbidden to walk under major flight paths'. The whole of Holland tuned in to watch their wedding.

In Group D, Iranian WAGs had a tricky build-up to the World Cup, when it was revealed that Iran's German-based superstar Mehdi Mahdavikia had two wives—one in Iran and one in Germany. 'Fortunately… neither of them was up to much,' the *Independent* said.

Portugal's Helen Sveden, midfielder Luis Figo's better half, made a strong showing. However, the prize was awarded to variety show host and actress Adriana Lavat, wife of Mexico's Rafael Marquez.

Representing Italy in Group E, Ilary Blasi, wife of striker Francesco Totti, was judged to be worthy of her married name. Radka Kocurova, who came second in the Miss Czech beauty pageant, was being scouted by the paparazzi after it was announced that her husband, Thomas Rosicky, would be moving to Arsenal. But the winner in Group F was thought to be Bianca Kajlich, the star of US teen soap *Dawson's Creek* and wife of the American player Landon Donovan.

In Group G, South Korea had Lee Hye-Won, a former Miss Korea, who, along with her Beckham-esque husband Ahn Jung-Hwan, was feted as a huge celebrity in her own country. But in the French camp, there was Claire Henry, the wife of the Arsenal ace Thierry Henry, who had made an appearance in the movie *The Fifth Element*.

Ukraine had an American import in the shape of model Kristin Pazik, wife of striker Andrei Shevchenko. In Group H she was up against Mamen Sanz, wife of the Spanish legend Raúl. While he was at Real Madrid, she became so fed up with her fellow WAG Victoria Beckham that she gave her a good slagging in the press.

The *Independent* then printed skybet.com's WAG odds:

33/1 Photo of two or more wives physically fighting with each other appear in press during World Cup

10/1 England wives' bar bill of over £10k spent in one single night appears in press during World Cup

6/4 Posh to appear on live TV during England game without shades on

100/1 Coleen to break a metatarsal

14/1 Victoria Beckham and Cheryl Tweedy to record a number one single together (by end 2006)

20/1 Joe Cole and Abigail Clancy publicly declare they're a couple by end 2006

100/1 Ashley Cole and Cheryl Tweedy's first child

to be called Baden-Baden

100/1 Hotel manager announces pool has been turned orange by WAGs' fake tan

8/1 Posh to be bridesmaid at Cheryl's wedding

8/1 WAGs to release workout DVD

33/1 Sven and Nancy announce engagement before the end of the World Cup

10/1 Photo of a WAG dancing topless on the table in a German bar to appear in UK press during World Cup.

Showing more restraint, the *News of the World* concentrated on Vanessa Perroncel's bump. She was eighteen weeks pregnant. Wayne Bridge's told the newspaper: 'It's really fantastic news and we are both very excited about it.'

After England's match against Sweden in Cologne's Rheinenergie Stadion, the WAGs found themselves stuck in traffic on a coach for two hours on the way to Cologne airport. Told their private jet would be delayed by an hour with refuelling problems and that they had to wait with no food or water in stifling heat and humidity, Victoria Beckham blew her top.

'A dog gets better treatment than this. It is the middle of the night, we have children and pregnant women and we have been waiting for hours,' she bellowed at a hapless FA official.

They got back to their hotel in Baden-Baden long

after those who had taken trains or coaches all the way.

After England beat Ecuador, Tortora Carmine, owner of the Garibaldi—which the *Sun* called 'Baden-Baden's answer to London's trendy Met Bar'—ordered another 1,232 pints of strong lager.

'I've still got a few hundred bottles of champagne on ice, which should last a few days,' he said.

He was full of praise for the WAGs who had made his bar one of the most famous in the world.

'I don't even mind them dancing on the tables—their stilettos haven't left any scratches,' he said.

In the run-up to England's quarter final match against Portugal, the WAGs were ferried to England's Buhlerhohe Schlosshotel base for a barbecue and were allowed to stay over for 'a night of nookie,' as the *Sun* put it.

By that time, the *Daily Star* estimated that the WAGs had spent £1 million between them on shopping and partying, including Victoria Beckham's £4,783 first-class airline day return to Canada for a business meeting. A posse of WAGs, led by Coleen, Cheryl and Carly, blew thousands on designer watches. The group are said to have emptied Baden-Baden's jewellery stores of exclusive watches by top designers Frank Muller and Rolex—estimated cost £616,000.

England was knocked out by Portugal in a penalty shoot-out in Gelsenkirchen. The WAGs hugged each other, while Coleen McLoughlin sobbed after Wayne

Rooney was sent off. However, there was another incident on the way back to Baden-Baden. Their coach pulled over at a motorway service station. Carly Zucker and Toni Poole got out of the bus looking upset. Vanessa Perroncel stepped out too.

The following day, the WAGs checked out of the Brenner Park hotel having run up a bill of £250,000. According to the *Sunday Mirror*, the staff were happy to see the back of them. One staff member said the novelty of having the hard-partying women staying in the hotel had long since worn off.

Having done sterling service in Germany, Vanessa Perroncel gave birth to a son, Jaydon, on 21 November 2006. She and Wayne parted company in 2009. But she was back in the headlines the following year over a super-injunction John Terry had tried to take out preventing the *News of the World* reporting allegations that Terry had had a four-month affair in late 2009 with her. Terry had married Toni Poole at Blenheim Palace in 2007 in a £1-million ceremony which was largely funded by a lucrative deal with *OK!* magazine. Chelsea and England teammate Wayne Bridge and Vanessa Perroncel were among the guests at the wedding.

Before the wedding Terry said: 'I've misbehaved and slept with girls behind her back and that's not right. She knows about it all now and we're moving on. I'm not going to cheat on her ever again.'

It seems that WAGs' partners were more interested

in sh***ing-sh***ing than shopping-shopping.

When the injunction was denied, the tabloid press had a field day. As a result, Terry was dropped as England's captain and when Chelsea played Manchester United, which Bridge had transferred to in 2009, Bridge refused to shake his hand. Wayne then quit international football before the 2010 World Cup in South Africa where they would have been in the squad together. He said his place in the squad was 'untenable and potentially divisive'.

However, the *News of the World* and the *Mail on Sunday* subsequently printed similarly worded retractions. The longer one in the *News of the World* said: 'On January 31 and afterwards we published some personal information about Vanessa Perroncel in articles concerning an alleged affair with the footballer John Terry. Miss Perroncel has since informed us that she would have preferred her personal information to remain private and it was untrue in any case. We apologise to Miss Perroncel for any distress caused.'

She told the *Guardian*: 'It is like a nightmare. Every day you think: 'What else are they going to say about me?' It is so intrusive and so false. Every day, so many lies—and then people making judgments because of the lies.'

On 25 March 2010, the High Court ordered Bridge to pay Vanessa £6,000 a month for the maintenance of his son Jaydon until he was eighteen. Four years later

Bridge married Frankie Sandford, singer with The Saturdays. But he had another run-in with his ex in 2016 when he became a contestant on, *I'm a Celebrity... Get Me Out of Here!* without telling her.

According to the *Sun*: 'Vanessa was offered the jungle six years ago and refused. When she texted Wayne to ask him if it was true or not, he told her to ignore the gossip.'

She had been offered parts in a number of shows, including *I'm a Celebrity...* but had turned them down.

Meanwhile there was more trouble in the Terry fold. There was speculation that John's brother Paul, a midfielder with Rushden and Diamonds, had an affair with Lindsay Cowan, the fiancée of teammate Dale Roberts who subsequently committed suicide.

20
War of the Wags

Wayne Rooney succeeded John Terry as England's captain in 2014. He had married Coleen Rooney in 2008. They had been together for six years, beginning their relationship at the age of sixteen. The wedding took place in Portofino and the couple were paid a reported record-setting £2.5 million by *OK!* magazine for exclusive coverage. Coleen arranged for his favourite band, the *Stereophonics*, to play at the reception, along with her favourite band *Westlife*. The wedding reportedly cost £20 million.

The couple had four sons. They moved into a £1.3-million mansion in Formby, then a £4-million Georgian pile in Cheshire. But their relationship had not always been plain sailing. In 2004, Rooney admitted visiting massage parlours and prostitutes.

'I now regret it deeply and hope people may understand that it was the sort of mistake you make when you are young and stupid,' he said in a statement. 'It was at a time when I was very young and immature and before I had settled down with Coleen.' It was subsequently revealed in the press that there had been other women, some older and some in fancy dress and some who had previously had passionate nights with other Manchester player.

But it was not all one-sided. In April 2006, Rooney scored when he was awarded £100,000 in libel damages from the *Sun* and *News of the World*, who had claimed that he had assaulted Coleen in a nightclub. Rooney donated the money to charity.

Then in September 2017 Rooney was stopped by the police for drunken driving. In the car with him was twenty-nine-year-old blonde Laura Simpson who he had met at the Symposium bar in Wilmslow. She claimed the footballer ogled her breasts before they had a 'kiss'. Coleen, who was pregnant with their fourth child at the time moved to her parents' house but returned home two days later.

Meanwhile Coleen was breaking through the headlines instead of being chained by them when she carved out a media career of her own as first pioneered by Sheryl Gascoigne. She wrote a column for celebrity magazine *Closer* and a weekly fashion column for *OK!* She started as a TV presenter on *Tonight with Trevor McDonald*, then had her own series *Coleen's Real Women* on ITV. Then came the bestselling exercise DVD *Coleen McLoughlin's Brand-New Body Workout*.

After the publicity she garnered at the 2006 World

Cup, she was given £3 million to be the face of the label George at Asda. She got another £2 million for fronting the publicity for Littlewoods.com.

'The role is a perfect match in enabling me to select and wear my favourite styles as well as share my ideas on how to carry off the season's new trends,' she confessed to the media.

Her autobiography *Welcome to My World* was published in 2007, following by *Coleen's Real Style* and the four-book series *Coleen Style Queen*.

But where there is one Queen WAG, there will soon come another. In October 2019, hostilities broke out with Rebekah Vardy, wife of England and Leicester City striker Jamie Vardy. Former model Rebekah was a two-time WAG. She had been married twice before and had a son by Sheffield Wednesday defender Luke Foster, before marrying Jamie Vardy in 2016.

This led later to appearances on *I'm a Celebrity… Get Me Out of Here!*, *Good Morning Britain*, *Jeremy Vine* and *This Morning*. She and Jamie also appeared on *Celebrity Gogglebox* and, with the whole family, on *How To Spend It Well at Christmas*. She was also recruited for *Dancing on Ice*.

On 9 October 2019, Coleen Rooney tweeted, alleging that posts from her private Instagram account were being leaked to the *Sun* newspaper. So Coleen had set a trap. She restricted access to her Instagram feed to one suspect, then posted three bogus stories on the platform—about her plans to return to TV, the basement of the Rooneys' new house being flooded and visiting a clinic in Mexico to choose the gender of her fifth child.

When the *Sun* contacted Coleen to verify the details, she refused to comment. She then went back on social to reveal the one suspect that she had not blocked.

Coleen posted: 'I have saved and screenshotted all the original stories which clearly show just one person has viewed them. It's .... Rebekah Vardy's account.' It stung.

This went out to her 1.2 million Twitter followers and her 885,000 followers on Instagram. Her dogged sleuthing earned her the nickname 'WAGatha Christie', after famed detective novelist Agatha Christie. Impressed, Channel Four newsreader Krishan Guru Murthy called in her help with the Brexit leaks plaguing Johnson's government: 'Can we get Coleen Rooney to find the 'source' in No 10?' And, going a step further towards unpicking the country's Rubik's cube, comedian Nish Kumar suggested: 'Get Coleen to solve Brexit.'

Love Island star Chris Hughes commented: 'This is the best detective work since Columbo aired in February 1968. Feel for Coleen.'

Pointless host Richard Osman added: 'I will vote for any political party who agree to immediately give us the rest of the day off so we can follow this Coleen

Rooney/Rebekah Vardy thing properly.'

However, the *Sun*, usually not shy of an opinion, refused to take sides. It said: 'Like all reputable media organisations, we don't comment on sources.'

Rebekah took the accusations amiss. She phoned Coleen sobbing and begging her to believe she wasn't at fault. It was high drama at the almost WAG coral.

She claimed that her own Instagram account had been hacked and tweeted: 'As I have just said to you on the phone, I wish you had called me if you thought this. I never speak to anyone about you as various journalists who have asked me to over the years can vouch for. If you thought this was happening, you could have told me & I could have changed my passwords to see if it stopped. Over the years various people have had access to my Insta & just this week I found I was following people I didn't know and have never followed myself. I'm not being funny, but I don't need the money, what would I gain from selling stories on you? I liked you a lot Coleen & I'm so upset that you have chosen to do this, especially when I'm heavily pregnant. I'm disgusted that I'm even having to deny this. You should have called me the first time this happened.' This was followed by a broken heart emoji.

Things went from bad to worse. In the resulting Twitter storm Rebekah slammed Coleen for inviting cruel trolls to bully her. One horrific anonymous post read: 'F**k you sly c**t I hope that baby dies you b***h.'

Rebekah reported death threats to the police and demanded that Coleen hand over the screen shot that allegedly proved hers was the only Instagram profile used to view the private posts.

When the two WAGs failed to patch it up, Rebekah launched a £1-million lawsuit for defamation with her lawyers claiming the incident had affected her physical and mental health. They also claimed that Vardy's husband faced abuse on the pitch over the matter which meant they couldn't let their young children attend games anymore.

At preliminary hearing in the High Court on 19 November 2020, Rebekah's barrister Hugh Tomlinson QC said Mrs Rooney's posts were an 'untrue and unjustified defamatory attack... published and republished to millions of people'. He said that while this had been trivialised in the media as the 'WAG wars... the impact on Mrs Vardy was not trivial'. Coleen's social media post made it clear that the person accused of leaking the stories 'is Rebekah Vardy, the finger is being pointed at her, as the villain, the person, the someone, the one person'. The knives were out throughout Britain her team concluded.

The backlash on Twitter led some social media users even to link Rebekah with the disappearance of Madeline McCann, and joke she was the new leader of the so-called Islamic State group. Jamie Vardy had become the subject of ridicule, with opposition supporters taunting things like 'Becky Vardy's a grass'.

The accusations had made Mrs Vardy feel suicidal, she had taken three trips to the hospital due to anxiety and had fears she would lose her baby due to the stress of the situation. Neither woman was present in court.

Coleen's legal team countered in a 55-page submission that 'there are reasonable grounds to suspect that the Claimant was responsible for consistently passing on information about the Defendant's private Instagram posts and stories to *The Sun* newspaper'.

While Coleen's defence claimed there were reasonable grounds to suspect that Rebekah was responsible, David Sherbourne, representing Coleen, said the message readers would take away from Mrs Rooney's tweet was 'it was Rebekah Vardy's account that was the source of private stories about the defendant appearing in the *Sun*—not Rebekah Vardy herself'.

He added: 'The fact that these sting operation stories also then appeared in the *Sun*... is the reason why the defendant published the post which is the subject of this claim.'

The judge ruled, however, that Coleen's post clearly accused Rebekah of being 'guilty of a serious and consistent breach of trust', while Coleen's lawyers had argued that the fine print in the Tweet was important and the use of three ellipses ('...') and the word 'account' meant she was not implying that Rebekah was personally responsible for the leak.

Mr Justice Warby thus found in favour of Rebekah that Coleen's tweet had been aimed at Vardy and not just her Instagram account. Coleen was ordered to pay Rebekah £23,000 in the court's costs of establishing the 'natural' meaning of her tweet.

In December in court documents Rebekah Vardy admitted staging pictures of herself with members of the paparazzi and taking a cut of the money. But her lawyers also alleged that, Coleen had sent her a warning 'If you play games with me, I will play them harder' and a message, on the birth of her child, 'congratulations on your brilliant news. Hope it all goes well for you x' to prove that her opponent knew she was in a vulnerable state. Did Rooney consider, they wondered, that it was others close to her rather than Vardy who might have leaked to the *Sun*?

The two sides agreed to a stay in the proceedings and the two WAGs were given until 8 February 2021 to seek mediation in their case without going to a full High Court trial. Both considered that £1m could be better spent elsewhere. Rebekah insisted that she was merely trying to clear her name. At Christmas she hinted that they could settle their legal battle soon. And during this time, she attempted to do some good PR on her image, making it to round 6 of the popular daytime telly show *Dancing On Ice,* appearing alongside the show's hosts—Phillip Schofield and Holly Willoughby.

She told *Hello!* magazine: 'The new year could potentially see a resolution between us. I'm pretty sure the public are sick of reading about it.'

However, in January the positions hardened as Coleen was said to be 'determined to see this through to the bitter end'. Yet just before their mediation meeting, on Zoom in order to avoid spreading COVID, Rooney offered to 'drop hands'. Each side would pay their own fees and donating to charity. All that Vardy had to do was admit that her Instagram account was the source of the leaked stories to the press and Coleen would accept that Rebekah didn't personally know about the leaks.

When the 4 February mediation did not work out as either WAG Queen had hoped for—Rebekah was reported to have declined a last minute peace deal—Master Roger Eastman, set 2 July as the date for costs and case management of the High Court trial. Master Eastman complained in March during a virtual meeting that the budgets set by both sides were 'extraordinarily large', while Coleen was reported to have said that her opponent's budget was 'grotesque'. The pair had to file revised budgets by 18 June.

On behalf of Coleen, John Samson argued that both sides should be ordered to hand over phones, laptops and iPads for forensic examination as this would reveal who had accessed Becky's accounts when and where from,

'In addition to data on the parties relevant devices, the defendant contends that the Court will benefit from data about the use of the parties relevant devices which is available on request from the social media platforms,' Samson said.

He added: 'The defendant's contention is that it will be important for the expert(s) to have the opportunity to examine as much relevant data as possible but also all relevant devices that are within the power or control of the parties and not just the devices or data of the parties to the claim.'

In conclusion, he pleaded 'claimant should not be permitted to prevent that by keeping essential data secret'.

Up to the hearing before Master Eastman, Vardy had spent £431,158 and she was budgeting for another £465,842. Coleen, meanwhile, had spent £181,000 and was budgeting for a further £402,312 on the trial itself. Vardy's lawyer's said about the difference, 'It has caused enormous distress to Mrs Vardy and led to her being targeted by hostile and abusive online messages, as well as causing extreme upset and anxiety to members of her family. It was necessary to take steps to seek to understand the allegations made by Mrs Rooney, which involved technical expertise, as well as to seek to resolve the dispute. Regrettably this was not possible and further costs have been incurred in pursuing the claim to this stage.'